THE MIRROR OF THE BLESSED VIRGIN MARY

(Speculum Beatae Mariae Virginis)

and

THE PSALTER OF OUR LADY

(Psalterium Beatae Mariae Virginis)

BY

SAINT BONAVENTURE

TRANSLATED INTO ENGLISH BY
SR. MARY EMMANUEL, O.S.B.

B. HERDER BOOK CO.,
15 & 17 SOUTH BROADWAY, ST. LOUIS, MO.,
AND
33 QUEEN SQUARE, LONDON, W. C.
1932

ALL RIGHTS RESERVED
Printed in U. S. A.

NIHIL OBSTAT

Sti. Ludovici, die 18. Maii, 1932,

Joannes Rothensteiner,

Censor Librorum

IMPRIMATUR

Sti. Ludovici, die 19. Maii, 1932,

✠ Joannes J. Glennon,

Archiepiscopus

Copyright 1932
BY B. HERDER BOOK CO.

Vail-Ballou Press, Inc., Binghamton and New York

PROLOGUE

There is no doubt, as St. Jerome remarks, that whatever is worthily said of Our Blessed Mother redounds wholly to the praise and glory of God. Therefore, for the honour and glory of Our Lord Jesus Christ, and ardently desiring to produce a work which will tend to the praise of His most glorious Mother, I have judged it fitting to take for the subject-matter of my treatise the most sweet Salutation of this Blessed Mother. But I acknowledge my utter insufficiency for such an undertaking. First, because of the sublimity of the subject; secondly, because of the slenderness of my knowledge; thirdly, because of the aridity of my speech, and, finally, because of the unworthiness of my life, and the supreme glory and praiseworthiness of the person whose praises I wish to sing.

For who is there who would not deem that subject incomprehensible of which St. Jerome does not hesitate to speak as follows: "That which nature possesseth not, which custom useth not, which eclipseth reason, which the mind of man is unable to compass, which maketh the heavens tremble, and striketh dumb the earth, which amazeth every inhabitant of

Prologue

Heaven, all this was divinely announced by Gabriel to Mary, and was fulfilled in Christ." Therefore I confess myself unworthy to speak of such and so great a heroine. Again I say, how could my slender knowledge and my dull mind suffice to conceive praises worthy of Mary, when the illuminated mind of an Anselm faileth in presence of the task? For he saith: "My tongue faileth, Lady, for my mind is insufficient. Lady, all that is within me burns that I may render thee thanks for thy so great benefits. But I am unable to conceive worthy praise, and am ashamed to put forth that which is unworthy."

St. Augustine, addressing Mary, says: "What shall I, so poor in talent, say of thee, when whatever I may say of thee is less praise than thy dignity deserves?"

Again, how can my untrained tongue, my arid powers of interpretation not fail in the praises of Mary, when Augustine, that most eloquent of men, says: "What shall we, so little, so feeble, say in praise of Mary, when, if all our members were turned into tongues, no one of us would suffice to praise her?"[1]

Again, if praise in the mouth of a sinner is unbecoming (Eccli. XV, 9), how shall I, a miserable sinner, a man of most unworthy life—how shall I dare to proclaim the praises of Mary, when I hear Jerome, a man of such great worth, hesitate? For he

[1] St. Augustine, *De Sanctis*, CCVIII, n. 5.

Prologue

saith: "I fear and tremble, all the while that I long to fulfil your expectations, lest I should prove to be an unworthy panegyrist. For there is in me neither sanctity nor eloquence, worthily to praise the Blessed and glorious Virgin." [2]

And again: "Why should I add to the sea a small cup of water? Why a stone to a mountain? And as Mary has already been so adequately praised by the tongues of men and angels, what can our puny efforts, and especially my own, add to these?"

Finally, St. Jerome, speaking of Mary, says: "If I am to speak the truth, whatever can be expressed in human words is less than the praise given by Heaven; for Mary has been excellently preached and praised by divine and angelic heralds, foretold by prophets, fore-shadowed by patriarchs, in types and figures, set forth and described by Evangelists, worthily and officially saluted by Angels." [3]

Having diligently weighed all these things, pious reader, I must beg your forgiveness for whatever insufficiency, whatever want of skill appears in this writing of mine. How shall I, so inefficient, succeed in a task before which Mary's unique and zealous panegyrist, St. Bernard, quailed? For he saith: "There is nothing which gives me greater delight than to preach on the glory of the Virgin Mother." And giving his reasons for this delight, he con-

---

[2] St. Jerome, *Epist. ad Paulam et Eustoch.*
[3] *Epist. cit.*

Prologue

tinues: "For all men honour, embrace, and receive her with the great affection and devotion that is fitting, yet whatever is said of one so unspeakably sublime, by the very fact of its being put into words, is less worthy, less pleasing, less acceptable." [4]

Yet St. Jerome encourages and consoles me, saying: "Although none can be found who is worthy to praise her, yet let not even the sinner desist from glorifying her with all his might." [5]

And St. Augustine, speaking of the manner in which the Son of God bestowed upon His Mother the gift of fecundity, yet took not away her integrity by being born of her, among other things says: "We who are so insignificant, cannot suffice to speak of so great a gift of God; and yet we are compelled to utter her praises, lest, by being silent, we should appear ungrateful. And certainly, that poor widow who made an offering so pleasing to God with her two brass mites, should not have withheld that offering because she could not give more; yea, rather by giving what she could, she pleased God exceedingly."

Hence it is that I, so poor in talent, and equally devoid of knowledge and eloquence, have presumed to offer to so great a Queen this poor script of mine, that in it, so to speak, as in a dim mirror, the simpler lovers of this great Queen should in some imperfect manner perceive who and how great she is. And be-

[4] *Serm. de Assumpt. B. Mar.*, IV.
[5] St. Jerom., *l. c.*

Prologue

cause this treatise is, as it were, a kind of mirror which reflects the life, grace, and glory of Mary, it is not unfittingly termed the Mirror of Mary. Oh, do thou, therefore, my most kind Lady and Mother, graciously accept this small gift offered to thee by thy poor lover! For with this puny gift, with this small work on thine own Salutation, I salute thee. On bended knee, with bowed head, with heart and lips, I salute thee, I wish thee blessing. Hail Mary, etc.

CONTENTS

MIRROR OF THE BLESSED VIRGIN MARY

		PAGE
I	On the Angelical Salutation	1
II	Freedom of Mary from the Threefold Woe of Actual Sin, from the Threefold Woe of Original Misery, and from the Threefold Woe of Eternal Punishment	5
III	The Meanings of the Name Mary	15
IV	The Name of the Blessed Mary Is Free from All Vice and Resplendent with Every Virtue	28
V	The Grace of the Blessed Virgin Mary Is True, Immense, Manifold, and Exceedingly Useful	37
VI	The Fourfold Grace in Mary—of Gifts, of Speech, of Privileges, and of Rewards	48
VII	The Nine Plenitudes in Mary, Which Represent the Nine Choirs of the Angels in Glory	63
VIII	Mary Shares All Gifts with the Lord	77
IX	"The Lord Is with Thee"	83

Contents

		PAGE
X	Mary the Daughter, Mother, Spouse, and Handmaid of the Lord . . .	90
XI	Mary for Her Own Sake and for Ours Is Fitly Compared to the Aurora	98
XII	Mary a Rod or Stem, and a Flowering Stem	114
XIII	Mary Compared to a Queen Entering into the Palace with the King .	125
XIV	Mary Is Blessed on Account of Her Fulness of Grace, the Majesty of Her Offspring, the Multitude of Her Mercies, the Greatness of Her Glory	133
XV	Mary Is Blessed by the Seven Virtues Against the Seven Capital Vices	149
XVI	Who and What Was the Fruit of the Womb of Blessed Mary . . .	160
XVII	To Whom the Fruit of the Womb of the Blessed Mary Belongs, and to Whom It Is Due	174
XVIII	To Whom the Results of the Fruit of the Womb of Mary Are Necessary, and of Its Twelve Advantages	185

THE PSALTER OF THE BLESSED VIRGIN MARY

Translator's Preface	201
Author's Preface	202

Contents

	PAGE
THE PSALTER	205
CANTICLES IN HONOR OF MARY	288
A MARIAN CREED AFTER THE MANNER OF THAT OF ST. ATHANASIUS	298
INDEX	301

CHAPTER I

ON THE ANGELICAL SALUTATION

Hail Mary, full of grace, the Lord is with thee; blessed art thou among women, and blessed is the fruit of thy womb.

HEAR, O most sweet Virgin Mary, hear things new and wonderful! Hearken, O daughter, and see, and incline thine ear! Hear that glorious messenger, Gabriel! Hear what is to be the wonderful mode of thy fecundity! Incline thine ear to a fruitful consent. Hear what is announced to thee as a certainty by God the Father! See in what manner the Son of God is to become Incarnate of thee! Incline thine ear to the Holy Spirit, who is about to operate within thee! Because thou hast ears to hear, hear!

And in the beginning of thy hearing, listen to this unheard-of salutation:

Hail Mary. This name, Mary, is not inserted here by Gabriel, but by the devotion of the faithful, inspired by the Holy Ghost. And the last sentence, *blessed is the fruit of thy womb,* was not uttered by Gabriel in his salutation, but was pronounced by Elizabeth in the spirit of prophecy. Let us each and everyone say, *Hail Mary*. O truly gracious and venerable, O truly glorious and admirable salutation! As Bede says: "Inasmuch as it is unheard of in human experience, so much more is it becoming to the dignity of Mary."

In this sweetest of salutations five sweet phrases are set forth, in which are contained five sweet prerogatives of the Virgin. Oh, how sweetly are these praises insinuated! For here is signified how most pure, how most full, how most firm and secure, how most worthy, how most useful was the Blessed Virgin Mary. She was most pure, because of the absence of all fault in her; she was most full and abounding, because of the plenitude of grace in her; she was most firm and secure, because of the Divine Presence within her; she was most worthy, because of the dignity of her person; she was most useful, because of the excellence of her Child. How pure Mary was because of the absence of all evil in her, is well expressed by the word *Ave*. Rightly is the word *Ave* addressed to her, who was ever entirely immune from the "vae" or "woe" of sin. Thus it behooved the Mother of God to be, as St. Anselm testifies: "It was fitting that the conception of the God-Man should be of a most pure mother, that the purity of the Virgin-Mother, than which, under God, there was none greater, should be hers to whom God had designed to give His Only Son, whom

He had begotten, equal to Himself, from His own Heart, that He should so give Him to her to be at the same time the Son of God and the Son of Man."

Again, how full of grace was Mary by the abounding plenitude of her gifts is well signified when it is said to her: *"Full of grace."* And truly full, and ever full, as St. Anselm testifies, when he most devoutly exclaims: "O Woman full and overfull of grace, of whose abundance every creature is revived and refreshed." Again, how secure and firm was Mary by the Divine Presence is well signified by the words, *The Lord is with thee.* Rightly is Mary safe and secure, when the Lord is present with her; for the Lord, God the Father, the Son, and the Holy Ghost, is with her, so that she is in an especial manner most intimately connected with God. St. Bernard shows this when he says: "Nor is God the Son alone with thee, whom thou dost clothe with thy flesh; but also God the Holy Ghost, of whom thou dost conceive; and God the Father, who hath begotten that which thou conceivest."

Again, how worthy was Mary, because of the dignity of her person, is well expressed when she is saluted in the words: *Blessed art thou among women!* For it could not be that her person, having been made venerable by such a blessing, was not most worthy. Therefore, St. Anselm, overcome with amazement, exclaims: "O Blessed and ever Blessed

Virgin, by whose blessing every creature is not only blessed by its Creator, but the Creator by the creature!" Again, how useful was Mary, by the excellence of her Child, is well expressed in the words: *Blessed is the fruit of thy womb!* For she availed to save the world, having brought forth the most excellent and powerful Fruit of salvation. Therefore doth the devout St. Anselm say: "By thy fruitfulness, O Lady, the unclean sinner is justified, the condemned sinner is saved, and the exile is recalled. Thy Son, O Lady, redeemed the captive world, healed the sick, and raised the dead to life."

You see, therefore, dearly beloved, in what manner Mary, because of her immunity from guilt, is rightly saluted with the *Ave*. Because of the abundance and immensity of her grace, she is rightly saluted as *full of grace;* because of the Divine Presence within her, and her intimacy with Our Lord, she is told: *The Lord is with thee;* because of the dignity and reverence of her person, she is rightly saluted as *blessed among women;* because of the excellence and utility of her Child, it is fittingly said to her: *Blessed is the fruit of thy womb.* We shall now treat of each of these points in order.

CHAPTER II

FREEDOM OF MARY FROM THE THREEFOLD WOE OF ACTUAL SIN, FROM THE THREEFOLD WOE OF ORIGINAL MISERY, AND FROM THE THREEFOLD WOE OF ETERNAL PUNISHMENT

Hail Mary, full of grace. Let us all utter this good and sweet word *Ave,* by which our redemption from eternal woe was begun. Let each one of us, I say, utter it; let all utter it most devoutly, saying: *Ave Maria, Ave, Ave,* and again a thousand times, *Ave!* Behold, *Ave* is said to the most holy Virgin Mary because of her absolute immunity from any fault; because of her perfect innocence and purity of life; rightly is *Ave* said to her in the very beginning of her salutation, *Ave* indeed and without woe [*"a"* or *"absque vae"*].

We must consider that the *"vae"* or woe, from which she is entirely immune, is threefold. There is the woe of guilt, misery, and hell. There is the woe of actual sin, of original misery, and the woe of the punishment or pain of hell. Of these three woes we may not unfitly understand what we read in the Apocalypse. "I heard," says John, "the voice of one eagle flying through the midst of heaven, and saying with a loud voice, Woe, woe, woe to the inhabitants of the earth!" Behold how each of these woes is multiplied by three, so that all together we have nine woes, against which *Ave* is rightly said to Mary. For there are three faults, three miseries, three hells in this woe, for the absence of which Mary is rightly saluted by the *Ave*.

First, the woe of guilt is threefold, *i. e.*, the woe of the guilt of the heart, of the guilt of the lips, and of the guilt of deeds. On account of these three woes it may be said: "Woe, woe, woe to the inhabitants of the earth!" Woe, therefore, to sinners because of the guilt of the heart, as it is said in Isaias: "Woe to you who are of a deep heart, that ye hide counsel from the Lord." Woe, indeed, to those who are of a deep heart unto evil, for the deep hearts of evil-doers are haunts of the devils, and sepulchres full of the filth of vice. Woe, therefore, to them, as is said in St. Matthew: "Woe to you, Scribes and Pharisees, hypocrites, who are like to whited sepulchres, which appear outwardly to men fair, but within are full of dead men's bones, and of all abominations." Oh, how far from this woe was the most innocent heart of Mary, as St. Bernard says: "Mary had no fault of her own, and far from her most innocent heart was repentance." Of what could the heart of Mary repent when she had never admitted into it anything worthy of penance? Therefore, her pure heart was not the haunt of the devil, nor the sepulchre of vice. Rather, it was a garden and a paradise of the Holy Ghost, according to that word of the Canticle of Canticles: "A garden enclosed is my Sister, my Spouse."—"A garden," says St. Jerome, "a garden of delights, in which were planted the seeds of all virtues, and the perfume of virtue." Because Mary was far from this woe of guilt, therefore it is rightly said to her: *Ave.*

Again, woe to sinners because of the guilt of the lips, as it is said in Isaias: "Woe to you who call evil good, and good evil." Woe to these, woe to all who sin by the lips, as is said in the Psalms: "The poison of asps is under their lips." Oh, how far from this woe was the most innocent mouth of Mary! Therefore Blessed Ambrose says: "There was nothing evil in the eyes of Mary; nothing prolix in her words, nothing forward in her deeds." On the lips of Mary there was nothing of the gall and poison of the devil, but the honey and milk of the Holy Ghost, according to the word of the Canticles: "Thy lips are as the dropping honeycomb, my Spouse; honey and milk are under thy tongue." Had not Mary on her lips this most pure milk when she uttered that most chaste word: "Behold the handmaid of the Lord"? Because the woe of the guilt of the lips was so entirely absent from Mary, therefore is she rightly saluted with *Ave.*

Again, there is woe to sinners because of the guilt of their deeds, as it is said in Ecclesiasticus

(II, 14): "Woe to the double heart and the wicked lips, and to the hands that do evil." Woe to the double heart, for the guilt of the heart; woe to the wicked lips, for the guilt of the lips; woe to the hands that do evil, for the guilt of their deeds. Oh, how far removed from such a woe was every deed of Mary and the whole of her life! Therefore St. Bernard saith: "It behoved the Queen of Virgins, by a singular privilege of sanctity, to lead a life entirely free from sin, that while she ministered to the Destroyer of death and sin, she should obtain the gift of life and justice for all."

Note that never did she contract the least stain either in thought, word, or deed, so that the Lord could truly say to her: "Thou art all fair, O my beloved, and there is no spot in thee." So, therefore, the most innocent and holy Mary was without woe in thought, word, and deed, and therefore is it said to her, *Ave*.

Secondly, we must consider that Mary was not only free from the threefold woe of actual guilt, but also from the threefold woe of original misery, *i. e.*, from the misery of them that are born, from the misery of them that bring forth, and from the misery of them that die.

The woe of the misery of being born is the woe of the weakness of concupiscence; the woe of them that bring forth is the woe of the pains of travail; the woe of the dying is the misery of being reduced to dust and ashes. Because of these three woes is it said to the inhabitants of the earth: "Woe, woe, woe to the inhabitants of the earth!" The woe of those who are born is the woe of the fuel of sin which is born in us, by which, according to our original corruption, we are so weak unto good and so prone to evil; so that each one is born with the *fomes peccati,* and by this is weak and wounded, and can truly say with Jeremias: "Woe is me for my destruction, my wound is very grievous. But I said, truly this is my own evil, and I will bear it" (Jer. X, 19.) But alas! not only is there in those that are born weakness and misery, inclining them, when adults, to actual sin; but also the woe of stain and of guilt, bringing them even as little infants under the wrath of God. Therefore the Apostle saith: "All are born children of wrath" (Eph. II, 3.) Oh, how far from this woe of them that are born was the most holy Nativity of Mary, who was not only free from original sin, but also from the fuel of misery, in so far as it leads to sin, for she was conceived without stain. Because the Nativity of Mary was so far removed from this woe, she is saluted by *Ave*.

Again, the misery of them that bring forth is that original curse pronounced against Eve, "Thou shalt bring forth children in sorrow" (Gen. III, 16.) On account of this woe it may be said to all who bring forth what the Lord said to some amongst them:

"Woe to them that are with child and bring forth in those days" (Matt. XXIV, 19.) Oh, how far from this woe was Mary when she conceived and brought forth, as St. Augustine testifies, saying: "Oh, how blessed is that Mother who without stain conceived Purity, and without pain brought forth Healing." Because she was so far from this woe of them that bring forth, therefore is Mary saluted with *Ave*.

Again, the misery of them that die is the woe of dissolution into dust, which was imposed upon man when it was said to the sinner: "Dust thou art, and unto dust thou shalt return" (Gen. III, 19.) Hence of those that are born and those that die, can be said that word of Ecclesiasticus: "Woe to you, ungodly men, who have forsaken the law of the most high Lord, and if you be born, you shall be born in malediction: and if you die, in malediction shall be your portion" (Eccli. XLI, 11 f.)

Certainly both just and unjust are born under the curse of concupiscence, and in danger of being reduced to dust; yet to the impious alone is this curse particularly addressed, for their concupiscence is more deadly and their dissolution into dust more odious; and to the wicked their evil inclinations are more hurtful, and the remembrance of their future dissolution is more bitter, than to the just. Oh, how far from this dissolution was the body of Mary, as we universally believe. For this body was the most holy Ark of God, to which corruption was unbecoming, but which, according to the likeness of her Son, should rise again, before any taint of corruption could infect it. Whence it is both of the Son and the Mother that the Prophet saith: "Arise, O Lord, into Thy rest, Thou and the Ark of Thy sanctification" (Ps. CXXXI, 8.) This Ark was made of incorruptible wood, because the flesh of Mary never became corrupted. Therefore St. Augustine well says: "The heavens were more worthy to preserve so glorious a treasure than the earth, and rightly incorruptibility followed on integrity, and not any dissolution or corruption." As Mary was entirely free from the misery of them that are born, so also was she from the woe of the dying, and rightly is she saluted by *Ave*.

Thirdly, we have to consider that Mary was not only immune from the threefold woe of actual guilt, and from the threefold woe of original sin; but also from the threefold pain of hell. This threefold woe consists in the greatness, the multitude, and the duration of the punishments.

Woe, therefore, to the damned and to those who will be damned, because of the greatness, the multitude, and the duration of their torments! "Woe, woe, woe to the inhabitants of the earth!" First, there is the greatness of the torments, as Ezechiel saith: "Woe to the bloody city, of which I will make a great bonfire" (Ezech. XXIV, 9.) The bloody city is the multitude of the impious, of whom there will be an immense bonfire made in the great conflagration of the damned. Oh, how far removed from this woe of greatness of torment was the greatness of the grace and glory of Mary, for whom, instead of the grievous torments of hell, was prepared by God so great a glory in Heaven, and as she was great and garbed in merit, so is she great in her reward. She herself is that great throne of which it is said: "King Solomon also made a great throne of ivory" (3 Kings X, 8.) Mary is the Throne of Solomon, great in grace and glory. St. Bernard well says: "As much more grace than others as Mary obtained on earth, so great a degree of singular glory did she gain in Heaven." Rightly, therefore, is it said to her, *Ave*.

There is also the multitude of the pains of hell. Isaias says: "Woe to their souls, for evil things are rendered to them" (Is. III, 9.) He says, evil things, in the plural, because there are many, yea, infinite evils rendered to evil-doers in hell. But to Mary, in contradistinction to the many evils prepared for the damned in hell, God hath prepared many good things in Heaven. No angel, no saint, can equal her in the multitude and accumulation of heavenly good things, as the Book of Proverbs says: "Many daughters have gathered together riches, thou hast surpassed them all." If we understand these daughters to be human souls or angelic intelligences, has she not surpassed the riches of the virgins, of the confessors, of the martyrs, of the Apostles, of the prophets, of the patriarchs, and of the angels, when she herself is the first-fruit of the virgins, the mirror of confessors, the rose of martyrs, the ruler of Apostles, the oracle of prophets, the daughter of patriarchs, the queen of angels? What is wanting to her of the riches of all these? St. Jerome says: "If you look diligently at Mary, there is nothing of virtue, nothing of beauty, nothing of splendour or glory which does not shine in her."

Now the pains of hell consist also in their perpetuity. In the Epistle of St. Jude it is said: "Woe to them, for they have gone in the way of Cain and after the error of Balaam, and have perished in the contradiction of Core." And a little further on: "to whom the storm of darkness is preserved forever" (Jude XI, 12.) Note that he says, *forever*, and think how great is the duration of these pains and of the darkness which will have no end. But against this eternal darkness in hell the Lord has prepared for Mary eternal light in Heaven, so that, as the sinful soul, the throne of the devil, will be miraculously dark forever, Mary, the Mediatrix, the throne of Christ, will be marvellously luminous forever according to the Psalm: "Her throne is as the sun in my sight, and as the moon perfect for ever" (Ps. LXXXVIII, 38.)

Thus, therefore, as the Most Blessed Virgin Mary was free from the threefold woe of hell, yea, from all the nine woes, rightly is it said to her, *Ave*. Let every one of us salute her with *Ave*, and let us petition her that, through her own sweet *Ave*, she will pray that we may all be delivered from every woe by our Lord Jesus Christ, her Son.

CHAPTER III

THE MEANINGS OF THE NAME MARY

Ave Maria. As we have said above, this name was inserted here not by the Angel, but by the devotion of the faithful. The Blessed Evangelist Luke says significantly: "And the name of the Virgin was Mary" (Luke I, 27.) This most holy, sweet, and worthy name was eminently fitting to so holy, sweet, and worthy a virgin. For *Mary* means a bitter sea, star of the sea, the illuminated or illuminatrix. *Mary* is interpreted *lady*. Mary is a bitter sea to the demons; to men she is the star of the sea; to the angels she is illuminatrix, and to all creatures she is lady.

Mary is interpreted: "a bitter sea"; this is excellently suited to her power against the demons. Note in what way Mary is a sea, and in what way she is bitter, and how she is at once a sea and bitter. Mary is a sea by the abundant overflow of her graces; and Mary is a bitter sea by submerging the devil. Mary is indeed a sea by the superabounding Passion of her Son; Mary is a bitter sea by her power over the devil, in which he is, as it were, submerged and drowned.

Consider, first, that Mary is called a sea because of the abundance of her graces. It is written in Ecclesiasticus: "All rivers flow into the sea" (I, 7.) The rivers are the graces of the Holy Ghost, wherefore Jesus saith: "He who believeth in Me, out of his belly shall flow rivers of living water." This He said of the Spirit, which they were about to receive (John VII, 38.) All the rivers flow into the sea because the graces of all the saints flow into Mary. For the river of the grace of the angels enters into Mary; and the river of the grace of the patriarchs enters into Mary; and the river of the grace of the Apostles enters into Mary; and the river of the grace of the martyrs enters into Mary; and the river of the grace of the confessors enters into Mary; and the river of the grace of the virgins enters into Mary. All rivers enter into the sea, that is, all graces enter into Mary. Therefore, she above all can say that word of Ecclesiasticus: "In me is all grace of the way and of the truth, and in me is all hope of life and of virtue" (XXIV, 25.) What wonder if all grace flowed into Mary, through whom such grace flowed forth upon all! For St. Augustine says: "Mary, thou art full of grace, which thou hast found with the Lord and hast merited to pour forth upon the whole world."

Consider, secondly, that Mary in the Passion of her Son was filled with bitterness when the sword of sorrow passed through her soul. Well could she say with Ruth: "Call me not Noëmi, that is fair, but call me Mara, that is bitter, for the Most High hath filled me exceedingly with bitterness" (Ruth I, 20.) Noëmi, who was at once beautiful and bitter, signified Mary, beautiful indeed by the sanctification of the Holy Spirit, but bitter by the Passion of her Son.

The two sons of Mary are the God-Man, in His Divinity, and man, in his humanity. Mary is the Mother of one in the body, of the other in the spirit. Wherefore St. Bernard saith: "Thou art the Mother of the King, thou art the Mother of the exile; thou art the Mother of God, the Judge, and thou art the Mother of God and of man; as thou art the Mother of both, thou canst not bear discord between thy two sons." St. Anselm exclaims: "O blessed confidence, O safe refuge, Mother of God and our Mother!" The two sons of Mary were both slain in the Passion; the one in body, the other in mind; the one by the bitter death of the cross, the other by infidelity of mind. And, therefore, Mary's soul was filled with exceeding bitterness, as St. Augustine testifies, saying: "That loving Mother crying out with intensity of pain, beating her enfeebled breast, had so fatigued her body and all its members, that, tottering in her walk, she could scarcely drag herself to the obsequies of Christ." Thou seest now how Mary was a sea of the Holy Spirit; thou seest in what manner she was a bitter sea in the death of her Son.

Thirdly, consider that Mary is a bitter sea to the devil and to his angels, oppressed by him, as the Red Sea was bitter to the Egyptians submerged in it, of whom we read in Exodus: "The Lord drew back upon them the waters of the sea" (Ex. XV, 19.) Oh, how bitter and full of fear is this sea to the Egyptians! Oh, how bitter and full of fear is this Mary to the demons! Therefore, St. Bernard saith: "Visible enemies fear not so greatly an immense multitude of hosts in battle array, as the powers of the air fear the name, the patronage, and the example of Mary; they flow and melt like wax before the fire, wherever they find frequent recollection of this holy name, devout invocation of Mary, and diligent imitation of her. Thou seest now in what manner Mary is a sea by the abundance of her overflowing graces, how she is bitter by the vehemence of the Lord's Passion, and how to the devils Mary is a bitter sea by the power she has of quelling them.

Now we must consider how Mary is interpreted "Star of the sea." This name is most suitable to Mary, for she fulfils the office that a star does to mariners at sea. We read, and it is true, that sailors, when they propose to sail to some distant land, choose a star by whose guiding light they may, without going astray, make their way to the land of their desire. Such is certainly the office of Mary, our Star, who directs those who sail through the sea of the world in the ship of innocence or penance, to the shore of the heavenly country. Well, therefore, doth Innocent say: "By what aids can ships pass among so many dangers to the shore of the fatherland? Certainly," he replies, "chiefly by two. By the wood and by the star; that is, by faith in the Cross, and by virtue of the light which Mary, the Star of the sea, hath brought forth for us." Very properly is Mary compared to a star of the sea, because of her purity, her radiance, and her utility. For Mary is a most pure star, a most radiant star, and a most useful star. She is a most pure star by living most purely; a most radiant star by bringing forth eternal light; a most useful star by directing us to the shores of our true home country.

First consider that Mary is a most pure star by living purely and without sin. Therefore doth Wisdom say of her: "She is more beautiful than light, than the sun, and above all the arrangement of the stars, and being compared to light, she is found more pure." Some read here, "before" instead of "more pure," but either phrase is fitted to our Star. For Mary is indeed *prior,* or before, that is, she is most worthy, most great; Mary is purer than the sun, and the stars, and the light. For both in dignity and purity she surpasses the sun, the stars, and the light, yea, even every spiritual and angelic creature, of whom it is said: "God divides light from darkness," that is, the angels who stood firm from those who fell. Mary is prior to and purer than this angelic light. Hence Saint Anselm exclaims: "O Blessed among women, who surpassest the angels in purity, and the saints in piety!" Behold how Mary is a most pure Star by the purity of her life.

Secondly, consider that Mary is a most radiant star by emitting eternal light and bringing forth the Son of God. For she is that star of whom it is said in Numbers: "A star shall rise out of Jacob, and a rod shall arise in Israel." The rod is the Son of God, who is the ray of Mary, our star; this is that ray of whom it is sung: "As the ray of a star." St. Bernard says: "A ray from a star does not diminish its brightness, neither does the Son of the Virgin lessen the virginity of His Mother." O most truly blessed, O most truly radiant Star, Mary, whose ray has penetrated not only the world, but also Heaven, and even hell, as St. Bernard says: "She is that glorious and beautiful Star arisen out of Jacob, whose ray illuminateth the whole world, whose splendour shines forth in the highest, and penetrates even into hell." As Mary was a most pure star, by living most purely, so is she a most radiant one, by bringing forth the Son of God.

Thirdly, consider that Mary is a most useful star, by guiding us to our heavenly country, by leading us through the sea of this world to the grave of her Son, as to the gates of Paradise. She is as that radiant star which led the Magi most surely to

Christ. Mary is that star which in the waves of the present life is most necessary to us. St. Bernard says: "Turn not away thine eyes from the splendour of this star, if thou wilt not be overwhelmed by storms. If the winds of temptation arise, if thou strikest on the rocks of temptation, tribulation, look upon the star, call on Mary." Therefore, lest thou shouldst be submerged in the sea of this world, follow the star, imitate Mary. It is the safest of paths to follow her, as St. Bernard says: "Following her, thou strayest not, praying to her, thou shalt never despair; thinking of her, thou shalt never err; if she upholdeth thee, thou shalt not fall; under her protection thou shalt not fear; if she is thy guide, thou shalt not grow weary; with her favour thou shalt attain thy end; and so in thyself thou shalt experience how truly it is said: And the name of the virgin was Mary."

Mary is also interpreted illuminatrix or light-giver. For this virgin was wonderfully illuminated by the presence of the Lord, according to that word of the Apocalypse: "I saw another angel coming down from heaven, having great power, and the earth was enlightened by the glory of him. . . . The Son of God is the Angel of Great Counsel; the earth illuminated by the glory of Him is Mary, who, as she was illuminated by His grace in the world, is now illuminated by His glory in Heaven, that, being thus illuminated, she may become a light-giver in the world and in Heaven. Therefore, we must consider that Mary, the illuminated, is a light-giver by her example, her benefits, and her rewards. She giveth light by the example of her life, by the benefits of her mercy, and by the rewards of her glory.

Mary is the light-giver by the example of her most luminous life. For it is she who by her glorious life giveth light to the world. She it is whose glorious life enlightens all the churches. She is the lamp of the Church, enkindled by God for this very purpose that by her the Church might be enlightened against the darkness of the world. Let the Church, therefore, pray, let the faithful soul pray: "For Thou lightest my lamp, O Lord, my God, enlighten my darkness." The Lord hath lit this lamp most radiantly, and by this light he puts to flight the darkness of our souls. St. Bernard felt this when he said: "O Mary, by the magnificent example of thy virtues thou stirrest us up to the imitation of thee, and thus dost enlighten our night. For he who walketh in thy ways, walketh not in darkness, but has the light of life."

Secondly, consider how Mary is light-giver by the benefits of her gracious mercy, by which so many in the night of this world are spiritually illuminated, as the Israelites in olden days were by a pillar of fire, according to the Psalm: "Thou didst lead them forth in a pillar of cloud." Mary is to us a pillar of cloud, for she protects us like a cloud from the fiery heat of the divine indignation. She also protects us from the heat of diabolical temptation, as it is also said in the Psalm, "He spread a cloud."

Mary is a pillar of fire. What would become of us wretched beings, so full of darkness, in the light of this world, if we had not so lucid a lamp, so luminous a pillar? What would become of the world without the sun? St. Bernard says: "Take away this lightsome body, the sun, what will give light to the world, and where is day? Take away Mary, this Star of the Sea, and what remains save an enveloping cloud, the shadow of death, and the densest darkness?" Thou hast seen how Mary is a lightgiver by her most transcendently luminous life, thou shalt now see how Mary is an illuminatrix by her most resplendent mercy.

Thirdly, consider that Mary is also illuminatrix by her most resplendent glory, which illuminates the whole of Heaven, as the sun doth the world, according to Ecclesiasticus: "The sun giving light hath looked upon all things, and full of the glory of the Lord is his work" (XLII, 16.) The work of the Lord is full of His glory; the most excellent work of the Lord is Mary. This work, as it was full of the grace of the Lord in this world, is full of the glory of the Lord in Heaven. Thus, therefore, Mary, giving light by her glory, hath looked upon all things, because through all the angels and all the saints she spreadeth the illumination of her glory. What wonder if the presence of Mary illuminates the whole of Heaven, who also doth illuminate the whole earth? For St. Bernard saith: "The presence of Mary lights up the whole world, and the very heavenly country itself glows more brightly from being irradiated by the splendour of that virginal lamp." So thou seest how Mary is illuminatrix by her light-giving life and also by her resplendent glory.

Now we have to consider how Mary is interpreted *"lady."* Such a title well becometh so great an empress, who is in very deed the sovereign lady of the inhabitants of Heaven, of the dwellers upon earth and in hell. She is, I say, the Lady of angels, the Lady of men, the Lady Sovereign in Heaven, on earth, and in hell.

First, consider that Mary is the Lady of angels; for it was she who was foreshadowed by the Lady Esther, of whom we read that she leaned delicately on one of her handmaids, and another maid followed her mistress, bearing up the train of her garment. By Esther the Queen we understand Mary our Queen; the two servants, the lady of whom is Mary our Queen, are all creatures, men and angels. Oh, what a joy to us miserable men that the angels have their Lord and their Lady from among us men! Truly is Mary Queen of the Angels. St. Augustine, addressing her, says: "If I call thee heaven, thou art higher. If I call thee the mother of nations, thou art above this praise. If I style thee Lady of angels, thou art truly proved to be so; if I call thee the type or form of God, thou art worthy of this name." Now the soul of man is the handmaid who in this world follows its Lady, Mary. It follows her, bearing up the train of the garment of its Lady, that is, gathering up the virtues and the example of Mary. But the angelic intelligences are the handmaids on whom Mary, their Lady, as it were, leans in Heaven. She leans upon them by familiarly associating with them; she leans upon them most delicately by taking her delight in them; she leans upon them most fully and entirely by communicating herself in her plenitude to the angels; she leans upon them as one most powerful by commanding them. Mary leans upon all the angels by her power. St. Augustine says: "Michael, the prince and leader of the heavenly militia, with all his ministering spirits obeyeth, O Virgin, thy commands; by defending in the body and by receiving the souls of the faithful, especially by presenting to thee, O Lady, those who day and night commend themselves to thee."

Now consider how Mary is the Lady of men in this world. Of this Lady it is said in the Psalm: "As the eyes of the handmaid are on the hands of her mistress," etc. The handmaid of the Lady Mary is every human soul, yea, the universal Church. The eyes of this handmaid should be ever on the hands of her mistress, for the eyes of the Church, the eyes of every one of us, should always look upon the hands of Mary, so that by her hands we may receive some good, and that we may offer to the Lord, by those same hands, whatever good we do." For it is by the hands of this Lady we have whatever good we possess, as St. Bernard testifies, saying: "God would have us obtain nothing which did not pass through the hands of Mary." By the hands of this Lady we should also offer to God whatever good we do, as St. Bernard exhorts, saying: "What little thou offerest, take care to commend it to those hands most pleasing and worthy of all acceptance, the hands of Mary, if thou wouldst not be repulsed. Well for us, beloved, it is indeed well for us, that we have such a Lady, who hath towards us such liberal hands, and is so powerful for us with her Son, that every one of us may have secure access to her." The devout Anselm saith: "O great Lady, to whom the joyful multitude of the just giveth thanks, to whom fleeth the terrified crowd of evil-doers, to thee, O all-powerful and merciful Lady, I, an anxious sinner, have recourse."

Thirdly, consider how Mary is the Lady of the demons in hell, so powerfully subjugating them that of her we may understand that saying of Psalm 109: "The rod of his power the Lord shall send forth." The rod of power is the Virgin Mary. She is the rod of Aaron, flowering by her virginity and fruitful by her fecundity. She is that rod of which it is said in Isaias: "There shall spring forth a rod from the root of Jesse." This rod is the Virgin Mary, a rod of power against the infernal enemies, whom she dominates by her great power. So great a Lady, of such great power, deserves to be loved by us, to be praised by us, to be prayed to by us, that she may protect us against our enemies. St. Anselm gives us the example, when, speaking to this Lady, he says: "Thee, O Lady so very great, my heart desireth to love, my mouth to praise, my mind longeth to venerate, my soul desireth to beseech, because the whole of my being commends itself to thy protection."

Now thou seest how Mary is the Lady of angels in Heaven, of men in this world, and of the demons in hell. Also how Mary is a bitter sea, the Star of the Sea, the Light-giver, the Lady. Mary is the Star of the sea to converted men; she is the Light-giver to the faithful angels; she dominates all creatures.

Let us pray, let us pray most devoutly to Mary and say: "O Mary, Bitter Sea, help us, that we may be plunged into the bitter sea of penance! O Mary, Star of the Sea, help us, that we may be guided rightly through the sea of this world! O Mary, Light-giver, help us, that we may be eternally illumined in glory! O Lady Mary, help us that by thy government and empire we may be filially governed. Through Our Lord Jesus Christ, Amen."

CHAPTER IV

THE NAME OF THE BLESSED MARY IS FREE FROM ALL VICE AND RESPLENDENT WITH EVERY VIRTUE

Hail Mary. This most sweet and affectionate name, so full of grace and so noble, so glorious and so worthy, excellently befits Our Lady. For most fittingly is so loving a virgin named *Mary.* For she is *Mary,* in whom there is no vice, and who is glorious with every virtue. She is Mary, who was entirely immune from the seven capital sins. She was most humble in opposition to pride; most loving by charity in opposition to envy; most meek against anger by her gentleness; indefatigable by her diligence against sloth; Mary by her poverty was detached against avarice; against gluttony she was most sober by her temperance; against lust she was most chaste by her virginity. We can gather all these things from the Scriptures, in which we find the name of Mary written.

First, Mary was most humble. She is that Mary of whom St. Luke says: "And Mary said, 'Behold the handmaid of the Lord'" (I, 38.) O wonderful and profound humility of Mary! Behold the archangel speaks to Mary; Mary is called full of grace; the overshadowing of the Holy Spirit is announced; Mary is made Mother of God; Mary is set before all creatures; Mary is made the Lady of Heaven and earth; and for all that she is not the least elated, but in all she is deeply grounded in humility, saying: "Behold the handmaid of the Lord." Well, therefore, doth Bede say: "Mary never exalted herself by reason of heavenly gifts; as she became more and more acquainted with heavenly mysteries, she fixed her mind more firmly in humility, answering the Angel, 'Behold the handmaid of the Lord.' This is an example to many, who in honours and prosperity, in graces and virtues, do not humble themselves with Mary and with Christ, but grow elated with pride like Eve and Lucifer. But the humility of Mary was most certainly not in word only, but also manifested itself in deeds; not alone in the word of her official reply, but in the fact of her submitting to the legal purification; not alone in the word by which she humbled herself as a submissive handmaid, but also in the deed by which she humbled herself as guilty and a sinner. For she is that Mary of whom it is said in St. Luke: 'After the days of her purification . . . were accomplished.' O hard, unhappy pride! O proud and unhappy hardness of the sinner! Behold Mary, who is without all sin, submitted herself to the law of purification, and thou, a wretch full of sins, submittest not to the law of satisfaction."

See how Mary was most loving by her charity. For she is that Mary of whom St. Luke saith: "Mary rising up with haste, went into the hill country." She went that she might visit, and salute, and minister to Elizabeth. See how this visitation of Mary was full of charity. In the description of that visit Mary is four times named and her charity towards God and towards her neighbour is most fully declared. Charity to our neighbour should be kept and cherished in the heart, in word and in deed. Mary had charity to her neighbour in her heart, and therefore, arising, Mary went with haste into the hill country. What was it that urged her on to haste in this office of charity but the love that burned in her heart? We read that the shepherds came *with haste* to the crib; that Mary went *with haste* to render a service; and that Zacheus *made haste* to come down and receive the Lord into his house. Woe, therefore, to those who are tardy in works of charity! Mary, again, cherished charity to her neighbour in her words; she is that Mary of whom it is said: "When Elizabeth heard the salutation of Mary." Charity in greeting our neighbour and on all other occasions of charitable speech is, I say, to be cultivated. The Angel salutes Mary; Mary saluted Elizabeth; the Son of Mary saluted those whom He met coming forth from the sepulchre, saying to them: *"Avete,*

All hail!" Woe to those who, out of hatred or dislike, deny to their neighbour greetings of politeness. Woe to those who deceitfully salute their neighbour like Judas, when he said: "Hail, Rabbi!" Oh, how sweetly did Mary know how to salute! O Mary, deign to greet us by thy grace! And most certainly she willingly salutes us by her benefits and her consolation, if we willingly greet her with *Ave Maria*. Mary not only had charity in her heart and in her words, but she also exercised herself in charitable deeds. For she is that same Mary of whom it is said: "Mary remained with her about three months." She remained for the service and the consolation of Elizabeth. Therefore St. Ambrose saith: "She who came out of charity, remained at her post." As Mary in all things had charity for her neighbour, so above all things she had charity towards God. For she is that same Mary who said: "My soul doth magnify the Lord." The soul magnifies that which it loves and rejoices in. Therefore, the soul of Mary most befittingly magnified God and most securely rejoiced in God, because she so ardently loved God. Of this love Master Hugh of St. Victor saith a good word: "Because the love of the Holy Spirit burned in a singular manner in her heart, therefore the power of the Holy Ghost did wonderful things in her flesh."

Thirdly, see how Mary was most meek by gentleness, most patient in all adversity. For she is that same Mary to whom it is said, according to St.

Luke: "And he [Simeon] said to Mary His Mother: Behold this Child is set for the fall and for the resurrection of many in Israel and for a sign which shall be contradicted, and thine own soul a sword shall pierce." This sword signifies the bitter Passion and death of her Son. The material sword cannot kill or wound the soul, so the sharp Passion of Christ, although by compassion it pierced the soul of Mary, never dealt it a mortal wound. For Mary never killed the executioners of her Son by hatred nor wounded them by impatience. Now, if other martyrs were most patient in their bodily martyrdom, how much more so was our martyr, Mary, in her spiritual martyrdom? Of her noble martyrdom St. Jerome saith: "O marvellous patience and meekness of Mary, who was not only most patient while her Son was crucified in her presence, but also before the crucifixion, when her Son was reviled, as it is said in the Gospel of St. Mark, 'Is not this the Son of the carpenter and of Mary?' and a little further on: 'And they were scandalised in Him.'" Truly is Christ a carpenter, but the works of His hands are the sun and the aurora. Alas, how far from the grace of Mary most meek are they who are so peevish, so impatient, so irritable as to torment their neighbours, companions, and fellow-workers.

Fourthly, see how untiring and diligent Mary was by her assiduity in good works. For she is that

Mary of whom it is said: "They were all persevering in prayer in one mind, with the women, and Mary, the Mother of Jesus" (Acts I, 14.) Mary, by persevering indefatigably in prayer, gave an example, which it behooves us to follow, and not to faint. And if Mary prayed so sedulously on earth, why should she not pray most earnestly for us in Heaven?

Therefore St. Augustine well doth admonish us, saying: "Let us with all earnestness implore the patronage of Mary: that while we serve her on earth with suppliant ardour, she by her fervent prayer may deign to help us from Heaven." But see, our Mary was not only untiring and most diligent in the prayer of the lips, but also most earnest in holy meditations of the heart. For she is that same Mary of whom it is said in the Gospel of St. Luke: "Mary kept all these words, pondering in her heart" (Luke II, 19.) Mary was never idle or slothful, and therefore she not only occupied her mind in holy meditations, and her tongue in devout prayers, but also her hands in good works.

It was thus that Mary remained three months with Elizabeth. To what purpose? Bede answers: "That the virgin might render diligent service to her aged relative." Alas, how unlike Mary is the wretched sluggard whose mind, hands, and tongue are so often devoid of merit!

Fifthly, see how detached Mary was by her poverty. For she is that same Mary of whom it is said:

"They found Mary, and Joseph, and the infant lying in the manger" (Luke II, 16.) The poor shepherds found the poor Mother, Mary, and the poor Infant in the poor spot, not in splendid pomp, but in a poor manger. But if the Mother had not been poor, she would indeed have found fitting hospitality. While you diligently consider these things, you may realise how great was the poverty of Mary, of which St. John Chrysostom says: "See the greatness of the poverty of Mary, and whoever is poor, may receive thence great consolation."

Most certainly, whoever is poor willingly and freely for God's sake, or who is poor of necessity, yet patiently, can be much consoled by the poverty of Mary, and of Jesus Christ. Far from this consolation are those rich men who seek things so very different. Therefore Our Saviour saith: "Woe to you rich who have here your consolation" (Luke VI, 24.)

But the rich must not despair, because not only the poor shepherds, but also the rich kings, found the poor Mary and her poor Son, as it is said in St. Matthew's Gospel: "Entering into the house, they found the child . . ." (Matt. II, 11.) So also these rich ones found them who had brought gifts. The poor find this consolation by poverty; the rich by liberality. While the poor are conformed to Christ by poverty, the rich are reformed to the likeness of Christ by liberality.

Sixthly, see how temperate Mary was by sobriety. For she is that Mary to whom it is said: "Fear not Mary, for thou hast found grace" (Luke II, 30.) Note that it is said: "thou hast found grace." Never would Mary have found grace, unless grace had found Mary temperate in food and drink. For grace and gluttony do not go together. And it is impossible that a man should at the same time be pleasing to God by grace, and displeasing by gluttony. It is good, therefore, to seek grace and to fly gluttony. For St. Paul says: "It is best that the heart be established with grace, not with meats; which have not profited those that walk in them" (Heb. XIII, 9.) Note that it is said: "Thou shalt conceive in the womb" (Luke I, 31.) Never would Mary have conceived God in her womb if she had given way to gluttony. How far from the grace of Mary are they who so often exceed due moderation in food and drink!

Seventhly, see that Mary was most chaste by virginity. For she is that Mary of whom it is said: "The name of the virgin was Mary" (Luke I, 27.) We have as witnesses of the resplendent chastity of Mary: the Evangelist, Mary herself, and the Angel. For she was chaste in her virginal body, as the Evangelist testifies, saying: "And the name of the virgin was Mary" (Luke I, 27.) In her virginal mind Mary was even more chaste, as she herself testifies. For she said to the Angel: "How shall this be done, because I know not man" (Luke I, 34.) That is to say, I do not intend to know a man. But Mary was most chaste of all in her virginal offspring, as the Angel testifies, who spoke of her thus in St. Matthew's Gospel: "Joseph, Son of David, fear not . . ." (Matt. I. 29.) For from the time the Virgin Mary was divinely overshadowed by the Holy Spirit, her virginity was never dimmed, but was glorified in a divine and truly marvellous manner. By her Child she was approved, by her Child she was ennobled, by her Child she was enriched. By thy Child, O Mary, thy virginity was gifted, endowed, and consecrated. Therefore St. Augustine well saith: "Truly do we proclaim Mary to be both Virgin and Mother, for true fecundity glorified her virginity and undefiled virginity glorified her true fecundity. Her virginity was rendered more glorious by her fecundity, and her fecundity by her virginity." Alas, how far from the grace of Mary are they who are not chaste, who are enemies of chastity!

Now, since the sweet name of Mary is of such favour as we have set forth, rightly do we call upon her, according to that word of St. Bernard: "O clement Queen, may Jesus Christ, thy Son, bestow the gifts of His grace on thy servants, who invoke the sweet name of Mary—Jesus Christ, who with the Father and the Holy Spirit liveth and reigneth God for ever and ever. Amen."

CHAPTER V

THE GRACE OF THE BLESSED VIRGIN MARY IS TRUE, IMMENSE, MANIFOLD, AND EXCEEDINGLY USEFUL

Hail Mary, full of grace. It has been shown above, how Mary, because of the pure innocence of her life, is rightly saluted by the *Ave*. We have now to show how, by the abundance of her grace, she deserves the salutation "full of grace." Consider, dearly beloved, this grace, the grace of Mary, this admirable grace. Consider the truth, the immensity, the multiplicity, the utility of the grace of Mary. For the grace of Mary is a most true grace, a most immense grace, a most manifold grace, and a most useful grace.

First, consider the truth of the grace of Mary. Of this Gabriel saith: "Thou hast found grace," etc. (Luke I, 31.) That grace is true which is found with God who is the Truth. He says "with God" and not with the devil. For the devil offers the grace of an evil prosperity, that one may sin more freely. Holofernes, who signifies the devil, says: "Drink now, and sit down and be merry: for thou hast found favour before me" (Judith XII, 17.) He says, "with God," not with the world, because with the world, that is, with worldly men, false grace and false contrition are often found. Therefore it is said in Ecclesiasticus: "Open not thy heart to every man, lest he repay thee with an evil turn; and speak reproachfully to thee" (VIII, 22.) "With God," he says, not with men; therefore Blessed Bernard saith: "Let us seek grace, but grace with God, for with men favour is deceitful." Again he says, "with God," not with the flesh; for the grace or favour of the flesh is false, as beauty of body and such like. Solomon saith: "Favour is deceitful, and beauty is vain" (Prov. XXXI, 31.) For the Virgin Mary, so full of grace, condemned the false grace of the world, of the flesh and of the devil. Therefore did she find grace with God, true and pure, defiled by no base mixture, so that she could truly say with Ecclesiasticus: "My odour is as unmixed balm" (Eccli. XXIV, 21.) The balm of Mary is the unction of grace, which was most copiously poured forth on her. Therefore St. Bernard, speaking of the text, "The Holy Ghost shall come upon thee," says: "That precious balm flowed upon thee with such fulness and abundance that it overflowed abundantly all around thee." Balm is usually mixed, and thereby adulterated, with honey or oil. But the balm of the Holy Spirit in Mary was not mixed, for it was adulterated neither by the honey of carnality and worldly consolation, nor by the oil of praise and flattery. But because the grace of Mary was so true and pure, therefore St. Jerome well says of her: "Whatever was done in Mary, was all purity and simplicity, all grace and truth, all mercy and justice, which looked forth from Heaven." Whoever, therefore, desires with Mary to find true grace, let him approach with Mary to Him with whom it is found, with every desire, in all earnestness, with all the ardour of longing, as the Apostle exhorts the Hebrews saying: "Let us go with confidence to the throne of grace, that we may obtain mercy, and find grace in seasonable aid" (Heb. IV, 16.) And note that whoever wishes to find, must seek, and whoever wishes to seek, must bow down. Let him bow down with Mary in true humility, whoever wishes to find true grace with Mary. For it is said in Ecclesiasticus: "The greater thou art, the more humble thyself in all things, and thou shalt find grace before God" (III, 20.) Mary, because she truly humbled herself, found true grace, as it is said: "He hath regarded my humility."

Secondly, consider the immensity of the grace because of which Mary is called "full of grace." The grace of which she was full was certainly immense. An immense vessel cannot be full, unless that is also immense wherewith it is filled. Mary was an immense vessel, since she could contain Him who is greater than the Heavens. Who is greater than the Heavens? Without doubt He of whom Solomon says: "If heaven and the heaven of heavens cannot contain thee, how much less this house which I have built?" (3 Kings VIII, 27.) It was not indeed the house which Solomon built, but she of whom that house was the type, which could contain God. Thou, therefore, O most immense Mary, art more capacious than the Heavens, because He whom the Heavens cannot contain was borne in thy womb. Thou art more capacious than the world, because He whom the whole world cannot contain, being made man, was enclosed within thee. If Mary's womb then had such immensity, how much more had her mind? And if so immense a capacity was full of grace, it was fitting that that grace which could fill so great a capacity, should also be immense. Who can measure the immensity of Mary? Behold what is said in Ecclesiasticus: "Who hath measured the height of heaven, and the breadth of the earth, and the depth of the abyss?" (I, 2.) Mary is a heaven, as much because she abounded in heavenly purity, heavenly light, and other heavenly virtues, as because she was the most high throne of God, as the Prophet saith: "The Lord hath prepared His throne in heaven" (Ps. CII, 19.) Mary was also the earth which brought forth for us that fruit of which the same Prophet saith: "The earth hath given its fruits" (Ps. LXVI, 7.) Mary is also an abyss in goodness and deepest mercy. Therefore she obtaineth for us the mercy of her Son, as it were an abyss calling upon an abyss. Therefore Mary is a heaven, Mary is the earth, Mary is the abyss. Who hath ever measured the height of that heaven, the breadth of that earth, the depth of that abyss, except He who hath made her, not only in grace and glory, but in mercy so high, so wide, so deep? Therefore it is especially of her mercy that Bernard saith: "Who can search into the length and breadth and depth and sublimity of thy mercy, O blessed one? For the length of it will help all who call upon her till the last day; the breadth of it fills the whole world, so that the earth is full of her mercy; and the sublimity of it will bring about the restoration of the heavenly city, and its depth hath obtained redemption for them that sit in darkness and the shadow of death." *

Third, consider the manifoldness of the grace of Mary, of whom Ecclesiasticus says: "I, like the turpentine tree, have stretched forth my branches, and my branches are of honour and grace" (XXIV, 22.) According to Pliny and the Gloss, the turpentine tree is a large tree of Syria, and it has many and wide-spreading branches. The male tree bears no fruit, but only the female; this fruit is double, ruddy and white and of a pleasant smell. This beautiful tree, growing in Syria, is the Blessed Virgin Mary. For "Syria" means watered, and truly the whole life of Mary was watered by grace, for she

* *Serm. de Assumpt.,* 4.

grew in the healthful moisture of grace from the womb of her mother. What wonder if Mary grows in the moisture of grace, when without it every seed will wither? Whence it is said of the seed in St. Luke's Gospel: "And being sprung up, it withered, because it had no moisture" (Luke VIII, 6.) The branches of this tree, branches of honour and grace, are the virtues, and the examples, and the benefits of Mary. Many are the branches, branches of honour and grace, the merits of her abundant grace, her many virtues and good example, her many benefits and her mercy. In these branches the birds of heaven joyfully dwell, that is, holy souls, so that it can be said of them what we find in the Book of Daniel: "In the branches thereof the fowls of the air had their abode" (IV, 9.) Oh, how wide-spreading, how high are the branches of that blessed tree, the Virgin Mary! How wide-spreading to men, how long to the angels, how high towards God! In what way she extends to all the branches of her graces and her mercies St. Bernard sets forth, saying: "Mary has opened to all the bosom of her mercy, that all may receive of her fulness: the captive redemption, the sick healing, the sad consolation, the sinner pardon, the just grace, the angels joy, the Blessed Trinity glory, the Person of the Son the substance of human flesh! The fruit of that tree is that of which it is said: "Blessed is the fruit of thy womb." That fruit was ruddy in blood, white in death. Therefore the spouse of God, that is, the holy soul, saith as in the Canticle: "My beloved is white and ruddy" (Cant. V, 10.) This fruit is also of a pleasant odour to devout souls. John the Apostle had this odour in mind when he said to the Lord: "Thy odour hath roused in me eternal concupiscences." O soul, O soul, dost thou not experience the odour of mercy of this fruit? Oh, if thou didst inhale it, wouldst thou not run after it, as is said in the Canticle: "We run in the odour of thy ointments"? It is to be noted that it is not the male turpentine tree, but the female, that brings forth fruit. So that fruit of life, Jesus Christ, was brought forth, not by a man, but by a woman, a virgin. Well, therefore, doth St. Augustine say: "A virgin mother was chosen, who would conceive without concupiscence, and bring forth a man without a man."

Fourthly, consider the utility of the grace of Mary. It is said: "A gracious woman will find glory" (Prov. XI, 16.) Behold the utility of the grace of the gracious Mary; it is the finding of perpetual glory. Most useful was the grace of Mary both to herself and to us. Most useful, I say, was the grace of Mary to herself. For grace made Mary delightful, miraculous, and glorious. Delightful in her soul, miraculous in her Son, glorious in her kingdom. Mary was certainly delightful in her spiritual mind, miraculous in her virginal offspring, glorious in her eternal diadem. Grace, therefore, made the mind and the soul of Mary delightful with spiritual delights, as a spiritual paradise of the living God, like that word of Ecclesiasticus: "Grace is like a paradise in blessings" (XL, 17.) Truly she was a paradise of God in blessings of manifold spiritual delights. Of which St. Bernard saith: "What shall I say of the delights of the beauty of virginity, with the gift of fecundity, the mark of humility, the dropping honeycomb of charity, the bowels of mercy, the fulness of grace, the prerogative of singular glory?" Likewise grace made Mary miraculous in her offspring, miraculous in her conception and bringing forth, while miraculously the virgin brought forth, and more miraculously conceived and brought forth God.

Therefore is it well said of her: "Thou hast found grace with God" (Luke I, 30.) Of this name, St. Bernard, speaking to Mary, said: "Understand, prudent Virgin, how great and what special grace thou shalt find with God, from the name of thy promised Son." Grace likewise made Mary glorious, wherefore it has well been said: "A gracious woman shall find glory" (Prov. XI, 16.) O truly happy finder, Mary, who is so great in this world, so great in Heaven! No pure creature found such grace in this world, such glory in Heaven. And certainly she found both grace and glory with the Lord, for as it is said in the Psalm: "The Lord will give grace and glory" (Ps. LXXXIII.)

But the grace of Mary was not only most useful to herself, but also to us, to the entire human race. For the grace of Mary gathers in the evil, nourishes and fattens the good, delivers all. It gathers in sinners from guilt, fattens them by grace, delivers them from eternal death. I say, therefore, that the grace of Mary gathers in souls to mercy, gathers evil-doers into the Church. This is well signified in the favour which Ruth found when she collected the ears of corn left by the reapers, when she said to Booz: "I have found grace in the eyes of my lord" (Ruth II, 12.) "Ruth" is interpreted "seeing" or "hastening," and she typifies the Blessed Virgin Mary, who was truly a seer in contemplation and was swift in work. For she seeth our misery and swiftly bestows on us her mercy. Booz is interpreted as "strength," and signifies him of whom it is said in the Psalm: "Great is the Lord and great is His strength" (Ps. CXLVI.) Ruth, therefore, in the eyes of Booz, Mary in the sight of the Lord, found this grace, that she gathered up the ears of corn left by the reapers, that is, souls are gathered to pardon by her. Who are the reapers but the teachers and pastors? O truly great grace of Mary, by which many are saved and find mercy, who were given up as hopeless by their priests and pastors! Therefore St. Bernard saith: "Mary, thou embracest with maternal affection the sinner despised by the whole world, thou cherishest him, thou never forsakest him, until he is reconciled to the tremendous

Judge." Likewise Mary nourishes the good with the fatness of grace. Therefore is it said in Ecclesiasticus: "The grace of a diligent woman shall delight her husband, and shall fat his bones" (XXVI, 16.) Mary was indeed the diligent woman of whom Bede saith: "Mary was silent about the secret of God, but she diligently considered it in her heart." Who was the husband of this diligent woman, but He whom she had encompassed in her womb? Of whom Jeremias says: "The Lord hath created a new thing upon the earth, a woman shall encompass a man" (Jer. XXXI, 32.) The bones of this man are all they who are strong in the Church, that is, in His body. These bones, by the help of the grace of Mary, are fattened by the unction of grace. They are fattened, I say, by the fatness of the Holy Ghost, by which he longed to be enriched who said: "Let my soul be filled as with marrow and fatness." Oh, who can reckon how many souls by the help of Mary are nourished and fattened by grace? And who indeed can calculate how great in Mary herself was this fatness of grace, by which so many millions of souls are nourished? What was lacking to her who was the dwelling of all virtue and grace? St. John Damascene says: "Mary, planted in the house of the Lord, and fattened in spirit like a fruitful olive tree, was made the dwelling of every virtue." Likewise Mary delivers all men from everlasting death. This was well typified in Esther, of whom we read:

"The king loved her more than all women, and placed the diadem of his kingdom on her head" (Est. II, 17.) We read, therefore, that there was a twofold utility in the grace of Esther which she had with the king: one was that she obtained the royal crown; the other, that she delivered her nation, which had been condemned to death. So Mary, our Esther, obtained such grace with the eternal King that by it she not only attained to the crown herself, but delivered the human race, which was condemned to death. Therefore St. Anselm says: "How shall I worthily praise the Mother of my Lord and God, by whose fecundity I, a captive, was redeemed, by whose Son I was rescued from eternal death, by whose Child, I, being lost, was recovered and led back from the exile of misery to the homeland of eternal beatitude." O Mother of grace, make us sons of grace. Grant that by thy most true grace we may be gathered for the pardon of sin, nourished by the spirit of devotion, and delivered from the death of damnation! Through Jesus Christ, Our Lord.

CHAPTER VI

THE FOURFOLD GRACE IN MARY—OF GIFTS, OF SPEECH, OF PRIVILEGES, AND OF REWARDS

Ave Maria, gratia plena. We have still some things to say of the grace of the most sweet Mary. We will now consider the fourfold grace of her gifts, her speech, her privileges, and her rewards.

First, consider in Mary the grace of the Gifts of the Holy Ghost. To this grace Mary, giving thanks, could apply the word of Ecclesiasticus: "In me is all grace of the way and the truth." What wonder if she herself is the grace full of life and truth, who is the Mother of Him who was "full of grace and truth"? And what wonder if in that rod is so great an affluence of the Gifts of the Holy Ghost, in whose flower the Holy Spirit rested with such an abundance of His gifts? Mary is that rod, and the Son of Mary is that flower, of whom it is said in Isaias: "There shall come forth a rod from the root of Jesse, and a flower shall ascend from that root, and there shall rest upon Him the spirit of wisdom and of understanding, the spirit of counsel and of fortitude, the spirit of knowledge and of piety, and he shall be filled with the spirit of the fear of the Lord." On this flower was a great abundance of the Holy Spirit, which has overflowed into the whole Church, so that the Evangelist John says: "Of His fulness we have all received, and grace for grace." Now that such an abundance of grace has overflowed from this flower into the whole garden, how much more will it abound in the rod or stem of the flower, in Mary herself? Let Mary, therefore, say in all security, "In me is all grace of the way and the truth." Certainly the grace of the way and the truth consists in the aforesaid seven gifts of the Holy Ghost; it was by the aforesaid seven gifts that the grace of the way and the truth was in Mary. The grace of the truth set Mary in order in the truth above herself, below herself, in herself, and without herself. The grace, I say, of the truth set Mary in order above herself by the gift of Wisdom; below herself, by the gift of counsel; in herself, by the gift of understanding; without herself, by the gift of knowledge. The grace of the truth set in order the soul of Mary in truth above herself, in the most wise contemplation of things to be enjoyed; below herself, in fleeing foresight of things that were to be shunned; in herself, in her sure knowledge of what to believe; without herself, in a most reasonable discretion concerning all she had to do. The grace of her life set Mary in order in a good life with regard to the devil, with regard to her neighbour, and with regard to God. The grace, I say, of life set Mary in order in a good life; towards the devil, by fortitude; towards her neighbour, by the gift of piety; towards God, by the gift of fear. The grace of life set Mary in order in a most strong resistance to the devil; in a most loving kindness to her neighbour; in a most devout reverence towards God. This was signified by the Holy Ghost in a most fitting manner by the house which Wisdom built for Himself, having seven columns, which were the seven Gifts of the Holy Ghost. Whoever, therefore, feels within himself the beginning of a desire for the Gifts of the Holy Ghost, can find the shape of these pillars in this house, and he ought to desire these seven pillars with great ardour and much prayer. Likewise, he who desires the sevenfold grace of the Holy Spirit must look for the flower of the Holy Spirit in the rod. By the rod or stem we attain to the flower, and so to the Spirit that rests upon the flower. By Mary we approach to Christ, and by the grace of Christ we find the Holy Spirit. Therefore St. Bernard well says, addressing Mary: "By thee we have access to thy Son, O blessed finder of grace, mother of life, mother of salvation, that by thee He may receive us, who by thee was given to us."

Secondly, consider in Mary the grace of the lips, or of speech, of which it is said in the Psalm: "Grace is shed abroad on thy lips." Such was the grace of the lips in Mary that she could excellently be prefigured by Judith, of whom it is said: "There is not such another woman upon earth in look, in beauty, and in sense of words" (Judith XI, 19.) Truly there is not, nor ever was, nor ever will be, such another woman upon earth, as Mary was, in her glorious life, in the beauty of a pure conscience, and in the sense of words of a most skilled tongue. We shall clearly see the grace of the lips in Mary if we diligently gather and meditate the words of her lips as recorded in the Gospel. We find in the Gospel seven sentences, sweeter than honey, dropping from the lips of Mary, and indicating excellently the honey-flowing grace of her lips, as it is said in the Canticle: "Thy lips are as a dropping honeycomb" (IV, 11.) The seven words of Mary, spoken to the Angel, to God, and to men, are as seven wells of honey. To the Angel, Mary spoke the word of chastity and the word of humility. Mary had on her lips the word of chastity when she said in answer to the Angel: "How shall this be done, for I know not man?" This is a lesson to the unchaste, who have on their lips not chaste, but base and carnal words. Mary spoke to the Angel the words of humility when she said: "Behold the handmaid of the Lord, be it done unto me according to thy word." This is a lesson to the proud and arrogant, who neither think nor speak humbly of themselves, but have words of boasting and elation on their lips. Again Mary spoke to men the word of charity and the word of truth: the word of charity in greeting, the word of truth in instruction. Mary spoke the word of charity when she so affectionately saluted the mother of the Precursor that even the infant in that mother's womb exulted. This is a lesson to the rancorous, who will not only not speak charitably to their neighbours, but disdain to speak to them at all. Mary spoke the word of truth when, the wine failing, she said to the servants at the marriage feast: "Whatsoever He shall say to you, do ye." This is a lesson to those who will not only not speak good words to their neighbours, but urge them to evil deeds. Again, Mary spoke three times to the Lord. She spoke more to God than to angels or to men, for she spoke twice to the angels and twice to men, but three times to God. To God she spoke a word of praise, of loving complaint, and of compassion. Of praise for the benefits bestowed on herself; of loving complaint for the loss of her Son; of compassion for the failing of the wine. Mary had the word of praise to God on her lips, when in thanksgiving for that God had looked upon her lowliness, she said: "My soul doth magnify the Lord." This is a lesson to the ungrateful, who, alas, give such scant thanks to God for His benefits, and at times grow puffed up against God by these very benefits. Mary had the word of loving complaint to God upon her lips, when she said to her Son, after the three days' loss: "Son, why hast thou done so to us? Behold thy Father and I have sought Thee sorrowing." Here is a lesson for the indevout, who do not seek Jesus sorrowing, when by the withdrawal of devotion they have lost him for many days. Mary spoke the word of compassion to God when at the marriage feast she said to her Son: "They have no wine." Here is a lesson to the unmerciful, who are not moved to compassion by the needs of others, and who neither help their neighbours, nor draw them to God. Behold now, O Mary, our advocate, it is still needful to us that thou shouldst speak to thy Son for us, that many of us have no wine; we lack the wine of the Holy Spirit, the wine of compunction, the wine of devotion and spiritual consolation. Of which St. Bernard thus speaks: "How often is it necessary for me, O my brethren, after your tearful complaints to beseech the Mother of Mercy to say to her Son that you have no wine! And she, I say, beloved, if she is piously besought by you, will not be lacking to your need, for she is merciful, she is the Mother of Mercy. For if she had compassion for the shame of those whose guest she was, much more will she have compassion on you if you call upon her earnestly." Consider well, from what we have said, what power Mary hath with the King of kings, because of the grace of her lips, for it is written in the Book of Proverbs: "He who loveth cleanness of heart, for the grace of his lips shall have the king for a friend" (Prov. XXII, 11.)

Thirdly, consider in Mary the grace of privileges. Of this grace it is said: "Thou hast found grace with the Lord, behold thou shalt conceive in the womb, and shalt bear a Son, and thou shalt call His name Jesus. He shall be great, and shall be called the Son of the Most High." See how Gabriel, asserting that Mary had found grace, immediately specifies what that grace is, saying: "Behold thou shalt conceive in the womb." Oh, how great and how unheard-of in all the world that a virgin should conceive and bring forth the Son of the Most High! We can perceive in Mary seven privileges, privileges full of immense graces, granted to Mary alone by God.

The first privilege of Mary was that she was, above all men, free from sin and most pure. For she was so abundantly sanctified by grace in her mother's womb that it is believed she was never in the least degree inclined to the slightest venial sin. Therefore St. Bernard saith: "It behoved the Queen of Virgins, by a singular privilege of sanctity, to lead a life free from every sin, so that, while she brought forth the slayer of sin and death, she should obtain for all the gift of life and justice."

The second privilege of Mary is that, above all men, she was full of grace. St. Jerome saith: "On others grace was bestowed in measure; but the whole fulness of grace was poured into Mary." And, therefore, well doth this same Blessed Doctor, comparing the grace of Mary with that of the angels and preferring it, say: "It is to be believed that the glorious Virgin Mary merited greater privileges of virtue, and received grace praised by the angels."

The third privilege of Mary was that she alone was a mother and at the same time an inviolate virgin. St. Bernard, praising this privilege, says: "Mary chose for herself the better part. Clearly the better, because conjugal fecundity is good, but virginal chastity is better, but the best is virginal fecundity, or fecund virginity. The privilege of Mary will not be given to another, because it will not be taken away from her."

The fourth privilege of Mary is that she alone is the ineffable Mother of the Son, the Mother of that Son of whom alone God is the Father; wonderful above measure that so great a privilege should be granted to a creature. Of this privilege St. Bernard saith: "This is the singular glory of our Virgin, and the excellent prerogative of Mary, that she merited to have her Son in common with God the Father."

The fifth privilege of Mary is that she alone above all creatures was in the body most familiar with God. For, what was never granted to any other creature, nor will ever be granted again in eternity —she bore God for nine months in her womb, she nourished God from her breasts full of heaven, for many years she sweetly brought up our Lord, she had God subject to her, she handled and embraced her God in pure embraces and kisses with tender familiarity, as St. Augustine says: "No wonder, Mary, that God reigning in Heaven deigns to rejoice with thee, whom, when He was a little child born of thee, thou didst so often kiss on earth." *

The sixth privilege of Mary was that she alone, above all creatures, is most powerful with God. St. Augustine says: "She merited to be the mother of the Redeemer." He also says: "Beg for what we ask, excuse what we fear, because we shall never find one more powerful in merit than thee, who hast merited to be the Mother of the Redeemer and of the Judge. It is a great privilege that she is more powerful with God than all the Saints, as St. Augustine declares: "There is no doubt that she who brought forth the price by which all were freed, can above all others pay the suffrage of holy liberty." But what would it avail us for Mary to have such great power if she cared nothing for us? Therefore, brethren, we must hold it for certain, and incessantly give thanks for this, that, as she has more power with God than all the Saints, so is she also more solicitous for us before God than all the Saints. It is the same Augustine who teaches us this, saying: "We know, O Mary, that thou above all the saints

* *Serm. de Sanct.*, XXV, CCVIII, n. 11, appendix.

art solicitous for the holy Church—thou who obtainest for sinners time to repent, that they may renounce their errors."

The seventh privilege of Mary is that she, above all the Saints, is most excellent in glory. St. Jerome says: "Everywhere the holy Church of God sings, what it is unlawful to believe of any other of the saints, that the merits [of Mary] transcend those of all angels and archangels. This privilege—not, as it were, of nature, but of grace—belongs to the Virgin Mary." Behold how glorious is the privilege of Mary's glory that she, after God, is most exalted in glory. The glorious privilege of the glory of Mary is, that whatever after God is most beautiful, whatever is sweetest, whatever is pleasanter in glory, that is Mary's, that is in Mary, that is by Mary. It is entirely the glorious privilege of Mary, that, after God, our greatest glory and our greatest joy is because of her. St. Bernard says: "After God, it is our greatest glory, O Mary, to behold thee, to adhere to thee, to abide in the defence of thy protection."

These, therefore, are the seven privileges of Mary by which we obtain the life of grace. And therefore, we may implore Mary, as Abraham implored Sara: "Say, I beseech thee, that thou art my sister, that it may be well with me because of thee, and that my soul may live by thy grace" (Gen. XII, 13.) O Mary, our Sara, say that thou art our sister, that because of thee it may be well for us with God, and that our souls may live in God because of thy grace. Say, O our most beloved Sara, that thou art our sister, that, for the sake of such a sister, the Egyptians, that is, the evil spirits, may reverence us, that, because of such a sister, the angels may fight for us, and that above all, for the sake of such a sister, the Father, the Son, and the Holy Ghost may have mercy on us.

Fourthly, consider in Mary the grace of rewards, on which we have already touched in speaking of her seventh privilege. To this grace can be applied that word of Ecclesiasticus: "Grace upon grace hath a chaste and holy woman" (XXVI, 19.) The woman chaste above all women is Mary, the woman holy above all women, in whom is grace above grace, the grace of glory above the grace of the way, the grace of rewards in Heaven above the grace of merits in this world. This grace of the beatitude of Mary consists in seven gifts of body and of soul. Every glorified body has four glorious gifts: the gift of wonderful clarity, the gift of wonderful subtility, the gift of wonderful agility, and the gift of wonderful impassibility; and if every glorified body has these gifts, how much more so will the body which brought forth Him who is the Glorifier of all bodies? What wonder if her gift of clarity is the brightest in Heaven, who by the gift of holiness was so resplendent in this world that St. Bernard says of her: "While yet thou didst live among sinners, thou didst shine before God with such sanctity, that thou alone didst merit to approximate to the glory of the eternal King." Again, what wonder if by the gift of subtility she is most subtile, who by the gift of humility was most subtile in this world? Speaking to her, Blessed Bernard says: "Thou wouldst never have ascended far above all the choirs of angels, if on earth thou hadst not lowered thyself by humility below all men." Again, what wonder if by the gift of agility she is swiftest in Heaven, who by her gift of loving kindness was so swift upon earth? For in the offices of charity she went with haste into the hill country, of the swiftness of whose haste St. Ambrose says: "Whither would she, who was now full of God, hasten, unless into the hill country with haste? For the grace of the Holy Spirit knoweth no tardy delays." Again, what wonder if by the gift of impassibility she is impassible in Heaven, who by the gift of patience and equanimity was so impassible in this world that she never felt the slightest impatience or hatred when the sword passed through her own soul? For we neither read nor believe that the least sign of impatience ever appeared in Mary. St. Bernard says: "Diligently revolve in thy mind the whole of the Gospel story, and if thou discoverest in Mary the least sign of rebuke, of hardness, or of indignation, then thou mayest hesitate to believe in her virtue in other things, and fear to approach her."

If such is the glory of the body of Mary, what,

thinkest thou, is the glory of her soul? This blessed soul has three beatific gifts—the gift of wonderful love, the gift of wonderful knowledge, and the gift of wonderful fruition, or, to put it in a more modern way, the gifts of vision, fruition, and experience. But in whatever manner the gifts of Mary are expressed, it is certain that these gifts surpass those of all other souls. For if all blessed souls are endowed with these gifts in Heaven, how much more the soul of her who brought forth in this world the soul of the Beatifier of all souls? St. Bernard says: "She penetrated the most profound abyss of divine Wisdom beyond what could be believed, and as far as the condition of a creature is capable, she was united to that inaccessible Light." Again, what wonder if the soul of Mary is immersed in fecund love, what wonder if she is loving above all, who is above all beloved? Truly, before and above all; for St. Augustine thus addresses her: "The King of kings, loving thee above all as His true Mother and Spouse, is joined to thee in the embrace of love." Again, what wonder if in most delightful fruition is immersed the soul of Mary who was fed by the most blessed Fruit of her womb? St. Augustine says: "Mary in brightness of soul enjoys Christ, and His glorious embraces, always present, always beholding Him, always thirsting to see Him, she is ineffably nourished by Him." Therefore, as the most glorious Mary exceeds all Saints in the grace of the way and in the grace of merits, so she exceeds all Saints in the grace of glory and in the grace of rewards. Therefore, she is well symbolized by Queen Esther, of whom we read that, being led to the nuptial chamber of King Assuerus, she found grace and mercy before him above all women, and he placed the diadem of the kingdom upon her head. This is eminently suited to Mary, of whom St. Jerome says: "She is raised above the choirs of angels, that she may behold the beauty and the countenance of the Saviour, whom she had loved and desired with all the desire of her heart." This Queen Esther, the blessed Virgin Mary, at her Assumption was led into the bridal chamber of the King Assuerus, the Eternal King, of which incident St. Augustine, addressing Mary, says: "The Queen Mary, being led into the bridal chamber of everlasting rest, possesses the favour and grace of the King Assuerus, that is, the grace of the True King above all women, that is, above all angelical intelligences, and above all beatified souls, so that in Mary there should be grace above that of all the blessed. And in very truth the King of kings placed on her head the diadem of the kingdom, a truly priceless diadem, so delightful, so wonderful, that no tongue can fitly speak of it and it is incomprehensible to every intellect.

Now, therefore, beloved, you have seen with how great grace of gifts Mary is enriched, with how great grace of the lips, with how great privileges, with how abundant a dower of rewards. Let us, therefore, beseech this finder of graces that she may let us find grace with God, through Our Lord Jesus Christ, Amen.

CHAPTER VII

THE NINE PLENITUDES IN MARY, WHICH REPRESENT THE NINE CHOIRS OF THE ANGELS IN GLORY

Ave, gratia plena. It was not enough for the Archangel simply to commend the grace of Mary; he wished also to insist emphatically on its fulness, when he said: *"Gratia plena."* O truly full, and fully full! Gabriel had not yet said: "Behold, thou shalt conceive in the womb." He had not yet said: "The Holy Ghost shall come upon thee." If, therefore, before the coming upon her of the Holy Ghost, before the conception of the Son of God, Mary was full [of grace], how much more so afterwards? Therefore Anselm aptly says of her fulness and of the fulness of her gratitude: "She, being already a thousand times full [of grace], was saluted by the Angel, filled with the Holy Ghost, breathed upon by the divine plenitude." Well, therefore, is Mary said to be full of the illumination of wisdom, of the outpouring of grace, of the riches of a good life, of the unction of mercy, of the fecundity of a pious offspring, of the perfection of the Church, of the redolence of fair fame, of the resplendence of divine glory, of the joy of eternal gladness. Let us consider these nine plenitudes in Mary, which represent the nine plenitudes of the angelic orders in glory.

First let us consider that Mary is full of the illumination of wisdom and understanding. She may aptly be symbolized by that which is said in the Book of Proverbs: "My husband is not at home, he is gone on a very long journey. He took with him a bag of money: he will return home the day of the full moon" (VII, 19 f.) This is that Man of whom Jeremias saith: "The Lord hath created a new thing upon the earth, a woman shall encompass a man" (XXXI, 32.) The woman is Mary—a woman indeed in sex, not in corruption; a mother of virtue, who encompassed Our Lord in her womb, clothed Him with our nature. This Man—if indeed, as Josephus saith, it be lawful to call Him a man—has three houses. It belongs to imperial majesty to have three mansions in the palace, namely, a reception-room, a supper-room, and a bedchamber. The reception-room is the place for conversation and discussions; the supper-room, for food; the bedchamber, for rest. So our Emperor, who rules the winds and the sea, has His reception-room, which is the world; He has His refreshment-room, which now is the Church, and was of old, the Synagogue; He has His place of rest, namely, the rational soul of man.

But alas! this Man, the Lord of hosts, had been very far distant from His house of the world, His house of the synagogue, His house of the soul, for "far from sinners is salvation" (Ps. CXVIII, 155.) This Man was not in His house when Jeremias complained: "I have forsaken my house, I have left my inheritance" (Jer. XII, 7.) He took the bag of money with him when He hid the treasure of His mercies and His grace from the world. But lo! this Man came back on the day of the full moon—of that moon, I say, of which it is said in the Canticle of Canticles: "Fair as the moon." This moon, therefore, is Mary. The full moon is Mary full of grace. Well is Mary compared to the moon, because by the Eternal Sun she is fully illuminated with the light of wisdom and truth. Therefore, the name Mary is well interpreted illuminatrix or illuminated. For she, who is our moon and our lamp, was illuminated by the Lord, and she was the illuminatrix of the world, according to that prophetic word: "For thou lightest my lamp" (Ps. XVII.) In the fulness of this moon, the Man came back to his house, when Christ came into this world in the flesh. O truly wonderful fulness of this moon! Behold, if Mary was full of the light of wisdom, which she received from the Eternal Sun, before she conceived Him; how much more full was she, when she so wonderfully conceived this Sun, and so entirely received Him within herself! Well, therefore, saith St.

Bernard, when commending the fulness of the wisdom of Mary: "Heavenly wisdom built for Himself a house in Mary: for He so filled her mind that from the very fulness of her mind her flesh became fecund, and the Virgin by a singular grace brought forth that same Wisdom, covered with a garb of flesh, whom she had first conceived in her pure mind."

Secondly, let us consider that Mary is full of the outpouring of grace in her affections. For such was the inundation of grace, so great was its depth and magnitude in Mary, that she could well be called a full sea according to that word: "Let the sea roar, and the fulness thereof" (1 Par. XVI, 32.) As in the sea there is a gathering together of waters, so in Mary is a gathering together of graces. Therefore it is written: "The gathering together of the waters was called [Vulg. "he called"] seas" (Gen. I, 10.) It is also said in Ecclesiastes: "All the rivers run into the sea" (I, 7.) All the rivers are the gifts of the graces, which entered into Mary, according to that word of Wisdom: "In me is all grace of the way and of the truth" (Ecclus. XXIV, 25.) How full is this sea, how full of grace is Mary, St. Jerome declares, saying: "Truly full, because on others it is only bestowed in part, but on Mary the whole plenitude of grace was outpoured at once." This sea, therefore, being full, let us hear it roar against vices. Let the sea roar, therefore, and the fulness thereof, let the full sea, let the full Mary, roar. Let it roar against luxury, preach chastity, and say: "How shall this be done, for I know not man?" Let it also roar against pride, by humility, saying: "Behold the handmaid of the Lord." Let it roar against ingratitude, giving thanks and saying: "Behold the handmaid of the Lord. . . . My soul doth magnify the Lord." Of the fulness of this sea it is likewise said in the Psalm: "Let the sea be moved, and the fulness thereof." Let the sea be moved, let Mary be moved, let her be moved by our sighs and mortifications, let her be moved by our tears and prayers, let her be moved by our alms and our other acts of veneration. Let her be moved fully, I say, that she may pour out on us of her fulness. Let us note what St. Bernard says in speaking of her: "If a vessel full of liquid is moved, it is easily spilt, and lets drop its contents. So the Blessed Virgin Mary, if she is moved by our prayers, pours forth graces upon us."

Thirdly, let us consider that Mary is in very truth full of the riches of a good life. Of this plenitude we can truly say: "The earth is the Lord's." By the earth is signified Mary, of whom we read in Isaias: "Let the earth be opened, and bud forth a saviour!" What more lowly than the earth? What more useful? We all tread the earth under our feet, and draw from it the nourishment of our life. Whence have we food and clothing, bread and wine, wool and thread, flax, and all the necessaries of life except from the earth, and from the fulness of the earth? What, therefore, is more lowly, what more useful than the earth? In like manner, what is more humble, what more useful than Mary? She by her humility is the very least of all; by her fulness of grace, the most useful of all. For we have all that is needful for our spiritual life through Mary. Well therefore doth St. Bernard say: "Let us look more deeply and see with how great a depth of devotion He wishes Mary to be honoured by us who hath placed the fulness of all good in Mary, so that if we have any ground for hope, or for salvation, we should know that it is from her it springs."* Hear now the Psalmist: "The earth is the Lord's and the fulness thereof." The fulness of the earth consists in fruits and divers riches, according to the Psalmist: "The earth is filled with Thy riches." The fruits and the riches of this most full earth, Mary, are the works, the examples, and the divers merits of the most holy life of Mary. The Lord filled her with such riches and with so great gifts that it is said: "The Lord looked upon the earth, and filled it with his goods" (Ecclus. XVI, 30.) St. Jerome, speaking of this fulness, says: "It was fitting that the Virgin should be pledged with such gifts, that she should be full of grace, she who gave glory to the heavens, God to the earth, who restored peace, who gave faith to the

* *Serm. de Aquaeductu.*

nations, put an end to vices, brought back order to life, and discipline to manners."

Fourthly, let us consider that Mary is full of the unction of mercy and of the oil of piety. Therefore she may be signified by that woman who, having closed the door of her house and gathered together within all her vessels, they were miraculously filled with oil, according to what Eliseus had prophesied to her, saying: "Thou shalt take them away, when they are full" (Kings IV, 4.) This woman is Mary, who was called "woman" by her Son in the Gospel of St. John, where we read: "Woman, behold thy Son." The vessels of this woman are her affections and her deeds, her desires and her benefits, which in Mary are all full of the oil of mercy. Well, therefore, doth St. Bernard say of this oil: "No wonder, Lady, if the sanctuary is so copiously anointed with the oil of the mercy of thy heart, when that inestimable work of mercy, which God had predestinated from all eternity in our redemption, was first of all effected in thee by the Maker of the world. Let us, therefore, say to Mary: 'Give us of your oil.' Let us beg for the oil of her mercy in this world, lest we should ask in vain at the judgment." That the house in which the vessels were filled should also have been closed, is admirably suited to Mary, of whose spiritual enclosure Ezechiel says: "This gate shall be closed, and it shall not be opened, and no man shall pass through it; for the Lord God of Israel has entered through it" (XLIV, 2.) The gate of Mary was closed by the lock of virginity; no man had passed through it by way of conjugal embrace; the Lord God came forth through her by a singular manner of birth. But certainly, because for the multiplication of the oil, vessels not a few were collected from the neighbours; therefore by these vessels may be signified all those who have been partakers of the mercies of Mary. Who these are, St. Bernard declares when he says: "Mary has opened the bosom of her mercy to all, that all may receive of her fulness: the captive, redemption; the sick, healing; the sad, consolation; the sinner, pardon; the just, grace; the angel, joy; in fine, the whole Trinity, glory; the person of the Son, the substance of human flesh."

Fifthly, let us consider that Mary is full of the fecundity of the divine offspring. Of this plentitude we may understand that word of Isaias: "I saw the Lord sitting upon a throne, high and elevated, and the earth was full of His majesty" (Is. VI, 1.) That house on the throne of which God sits is the Blessed Virgin, on the throne of whose mind the Lord rested. O truly blessed and stable throne, as it is said in the third Book of Kings: "Thy most firm throne for ever" (VIII, 13.) This most high throne is in the intellect, raised up on the affections. It is also most high above men, raised up over men. On this throne, therefore, of Mary, on the throne, I say, of her mind, the Lord was seated, and the house of her body was full of the majesty of the Incarnate Word. Of this ineffable fulness St. Ambrose says: "Well is she alone said to be full of grace, who alone obtained the grace which none other ever had, of being filled with the author of grace." O truly happy house, full of so happy a fecundity! For St. Bernard saith: "Well was she full of grace, who both kept the grace of virginity and acquired the glory of fecundity." The Lord, therefore, sat on the throne of the mind of Mary by grace, and filled the house of her body with His majesty by His assumed nature. Therefore, it is said in the third Book of Kings: "The glory of the Lord had filled the house of the Lord" (VIII, 11.) Then saith Solomon: "The Lord hath said that He would dwell in the cloud" (*ibid.*, 12.) Mary, therefore, the house of the Lord, was filled with the glory of the Divine Majesty by the cloud of the humanity assumed by God—that cloud, I say, of which we read in Ecclesiasticus: "The healing of all is in the hastening of the cloud" (XLIII, 24.) And again: "Like the morning star in the midst of a cloud." For like the star in a cloud is the Word in the flesh assumed by Him.

Sixthly, let us consider in what way Mary was full of the perfection of the universal Church. The Church had and has diverse and marvellous perfections and graces in her various saints, in whose fulness it would seem that Mary abode, that she might truly utter that word of Ecclesiasticus: "My abode is in the full assembly of saints." Truly was the abode of Mary in the plenitude of the saints, while in her own wonderful perfection the fulness of the perfection of the saints was not wanting to her. As St. Bernard declares, when he says: "Rightly in the fulness of the saints was her abode, to whom was not wanting the faith of the patriarchs, the spirit of the prophets, the zeal of the Apostles, the constancy of the martyrs, the sobriety of the confessors, the chastity of the virgins, the fecundity of the married, yea, nor the purity of the angels." For it is written in the book of Ecclesiasticus: "And shall be admired in the holy assembly" (XXIV, 3.) On account of this, the abode of Mary is in the fulness of the Saints, not in the fulness of the impious; because Mary remains willingly with those who are full of sanctity, not with those who are full of iniquity. She not only abides in the fulness of the Saints, but abides in fulness *with* the Saints, lest their fulness should grow less. She takes hold of virtues, lest they fly; she takes hold of merits, lest they perish; she takes hold of demons and keeps them in check, lest they do harm; she takes hold of her Son, lest He strike sinners. Before Mary there never was one who could dare thus to take hold of the Lord, as Isaias bears witness, saying: "There is none that calleth upon thy name, that riseth up and taketh hold of thee" (Is. LXIV, 7.)

Seventhly, let us consider how Mary is full of the redolence of fair fame. As a field is full of the scents of various flowers, so is Mary full of the fair fame of fragrant sprinkling. Of her fulness we may understand what we read in Genesis: "Behold the smell of my son is as the smell of a full field, which God hath blessed" (Gen. XXVII, 27.) This field is Mary, in whom the treasure of the angels, yea verily, the whole treasure of God the Father is hidden. Happy is he "who sells all that he has, and buys that field." The full odour of this full field is the full fair fame of Mary, her full honour. Of this St. Jerome saith: "Because she was filled with the many odours of the virtues, there came forth from her a most sweet odour, rejoicing the angelic spirits." Of this odour she herself, glorying, could use the words of Ecclesiasticus (XXIV, 20): "I gave a sweet smell like cinnamon and aromatical balm." The good odour of Mary was like cinnamon externally, in the rind of her conversation; like aromatical balm interiorly, by the unction of her devotion; like myrrh, in the bitterness of her suffering. The good odour of Mary was also like cinnamon in her deeds; like balm in her contemplation; like myrrh in her sufferings. O truly rich, and exceedingly rich she who, besides other aromas, was so full of the odoriferous balm of the Holy Spirit that St. Bernard, speaking of that word, "The Holy Ghost shall come upon thee," says: "That precious balm flowed in on thee with such copiousness and plenitude that it overflows most abundantly on all around thee." Well, therefore, could God the Father say: "Behold the odour of my Son is as the smell of a full field," as though He said: "Behold the smell of my Son, the honour of my Son, is from the honour and the good fame of His mother." St. Jerome saith: "The maternal honour is His, who was born from her."

Eighthly, let us consider how Mary was full of the reflection or resplendence, as it were, the expression of the divine glory, according to Ecclesiasticus: "The work of the Lord is full of His glory" (XXIV, 20.) Above all, the most wonderful work of the Lord is Mary, of whom it is said in Ecclesiasticus: "An admirable instrument the work of the Most High" (XLIII, 2.) Truly a wonderful work, for a similar one can never be found. Whence it is said of it: "There was no such work made in any kingdom" (3 Kings X, 20.) None indeed in the kingdom of Heaven, none in the kingdom of earth, nor in that of hell; for there never was such a work in Heaven, on earth, or in the nether regions. For this work is full of the glory of the Lord, because this glory shines most fully in Mary, above all pure creatures. For after the humanity assumed by the Word, there is no work, no creature, in whom there is such scope for the divine glory as in Mary. For the Lord has through Mary glory because of the restoration brought about in Heaven, glory in the Redemption accomplished in the world, glory for the deliverance wrought in hell —this glory He has in the fulness of grace in Mary. Therefore, well does St. Anselm say: "I speak to thee alone, Lady; the world is full of thy benefits; they have penetrated hell, and surpassed the Heavens. For by the fulness of thy grace those who were in limbo rejoice in their deliverance, and those who were above the world have joy in their restoration." Therefore, full of the glory of the Lord is His work, Mary, because, as it is said in Isaias, "The earth is full of His glory" (Is. VI, 3.) Full indeed is the whole earth, full is Mary of the divine glory, which shines in her most fully. Rightly above all the aforesaid is she said to be full of grace, who is most pleasing to all who are not ungrateful, as St. Bernard shows when, speaking of the words, *Ave gratia plena,* he says: "Well is she fully pleasing because she is pleasing to God, to the angels, and to men; to men by her fecundity, to the angels by her virginity, to God by her humility."

Ninthly, consider how Mary is full of the joy of eternal happiness. Who is ignorant that she is of those of whom her Son said: "Ask, and you shall receive, that your joy may be full"? If, therefore, the joy of the Apostles, of all those who are reigning with God, is full, how much more is the joy of the Mother of God full and complete? Of this plenitude St. Jerome says: "Full indeed of grace, full of God, full of virtues, she could not but possess most fully the glory of eternal splendour." What wonder, then, that she has full and overfull joy and glory in the kingdom, who had grace full and overflowing in her exile upon earth? What wonder if both in Heaven and on earth her fulness was above that of every creature, from whose fulness every creature has life? Therefore St. Anselm saith: "O Woman full and overfull of grace, of the overflowing of whose plenitude every creature gains new life!"

Thus you see in Mary the fulness of illuminative wisdom, the fulness of overflowing grace, the fulness of a fruitful life, the fulness of helping mercy, of the perfection of the Church, of good fame, of divine glory, of eternal joy. Now, therefore, O Virgin full of grace, deign to make us, who are so empty, partakers of thy fulness, that we may at last attain to eternal fulness. By Our Lord Jesus Christ, etc.

CHAPTER VIII

MARY SHARES ALL GIFTS WITH THE LORD

Ave Maria, gratia plena, Dominus tecum. It has been shown above how Mary, because of the purity of her life, is rightly saluted by the *Ave*. It has also been shown how, because of the abundance of her graces, she is rightly called "full of grace." We have now to show how, because of a most special presence of God within her, it is rightly said to her: *"The Lord is with thee."* But tell us, in what measure, O great Gabriel, thou bringest tidings of a great thing to the great Mary from the great God! But tell us, in what measure, or *how* He is with her? Behold St. Augustine answering this question, as it were in the person of Gabriel: "The Lord is with thee, but more than with me. The Lord is with thee, but not as He is with me. For although the Lord is in me, the Lord hath created me; but by thee the Lord is to be born." The Lord, therefore, O Mary, but who, how great? The Lord of the earth and of all things in general, the Lord who is especially the Lord of mankind, the Lord who is thine in a singular manner, O Mary. The Lord, I say, of all creatures in general, the Lord in a special manner of rational creatures, the Lord esspecially of thy virginal court, O Mary. We must consider, therefore, that this Lord, who is with thee, is in general the Lord of all creatures. Judith says: "The Lord of the heavens, the Creator of the waters, and the Lord of all creatures" (IX, 17.) And the Wise Man: "The Lord of all things loved her" (Wisd. VIII, 3.) Therefore, the Lord of all things universally, of all things visible and invisible. This universal Lord of all things was in Mary in such a manner that He made her the universal Lady of all things—the Lady, I say, of Heaven, and the Lady of the world. St. Anselm saith: "The Queen of heaven, and the Lady of the World, to the Mother of Him, who cleanseth the world, I confess that my body is exceedingly impure." But lo! this universal Lord of all things is a most powerful Lord, a most wise Lord, a most rich Lord, a most unfailing Lord. A lord without power, without wisdom, without wealth, without permanence, would be a most imperfect lord. A feeble lord, one needy and insipid, or unable to keep his position, would be little esteemed. But Our Lord is universal, most powerful, most wise, most wealthy; His eternity is unfailing.

First note that the universal Lord, who is with Mary, is a Lord most powerful in will, and it is well said of Him: "All whatsoever the Lord hath willed, the Lord has done, . . . even in all abysses" (Ps. CXXXIV, 6.) Therefore, neither in Heaven, nor on earth, nor in all the infernal abysses, can anyone resist the will of so powerful a Lord, as Mardochai testifies, saying: "Lord King Almighty, in thy dominion are all things, and there is none who can resist thy will" (Esth. XIII, 9.) Behold, Mary, how great, how powerful is the Lord who is with thee! And because He is a most powerful Lord, He is most powerfully with thee: therefore, art thou most powerful with Him, by Him, through Him, so that thou canst truly say, "My power is in Jerusalem" (Ecclus. XXIV, 15.) Jerusalem signifies the Church triumphant in Heaven; it signifies also the Church militant upon earth. For truly both in Heaven and on earth the Mother of the Creator has power. How very powerful she is, Anselm recognises when he says: "Hear us, loving one; be with us, be favourable to us; help us, most powerful one, that our minds may be cleansed from stains and our darkness illuminated." The Lord, therefore, is with thee, O most powerful Mary.

Secondly, note that the universal Lord, who is with Mary, is a Lord most wise in truth. For He is the Lord, of whom it is said in the Psalm, "Great is our Lord, and great is His strength, and of His wisdom there is no number" (Ps. CXLVI, 5.) Oh, how wise is the Lord, whose wisdom nothing can deceive, nothing can be concealed from, because He knows all things. All our works, both good and bad, all our words, good and bad, all our thoughts and all our desires, good and bad, the Lord knows. Whence St. Peter says: "Lord, Thou knowest all things." Behold, Mary, what kind of a Lord, what a most wise Lord, is He who is with thee. And because the most wise Lord is most wisely with thee, therefore, thou too art most wise with Him and through Him. Thou art typified by that Abigail, of whom it was said: "She was a woman most prudent and most beautiful." Mary was so prudent and so beautiful that St. Anselm does not hesitate to say of her: "All the treasures of wisdom and knowledge are in Mary." The Lord, therefore, is with thee, O most wise Mary.

Thirdly, consider that the universal Lord, who is with Mary, is most wealthy in His possessions, as the Prophet testifies, saying: "The earth is the Lord's, and all that dwell in it." Not only is the earth and its fulness the Lord's, but also the Heavens and their fulness. For Thine, O Lord, are the Heavens, and thine is the earth, because "the heaven of heavens is the Lord's." Everything is the property of this Lord, Heaven and earth, bodies and spirits, all nature, all grace, all heavenly glory, all is the Lord's own. Therefore, the Lord is most rich, as the Apostle says: "He is the Lord of all, rich unto all that call upon Him" (Rom. X, 12.) Behold, Mary, how rich, how great is He who is with thee! And because the most rich lord is with thee so richly, therefore art thou most rich together with Him and because of Him, so that it can be truly said of thee: "Many daughters have gathered together riches, thou hast surpassed them all" (Prov. XXXI, 29.) The daughter Agnes, the daughter Lucy, the daughters Catherine, Cecilia, Agatha, and many other holy virgins and just souls, have gathered together riches of virtue and grace, of merits and rewards, but thou, O Mary, by thy universal riches hast surpassed them all. Oh, how rich is Mary in glory, who was so rich in misery! Oh, how rich is she in Heaven, who was so rich in this world! Oh, how rich is she in her soul, who was so rich in her body, that even St. Bernard exclaims: "O Mary, rich in all and above all, of whose substance a small part being taken, was enough to pay the debt of the whole world!" The Lord is with thee, therefore, O Mary most rich.

Fourthly, consider that the universal Lord, who is with Mary, is the unfailing Lord of eternity. Whence we read in Exodus: "The Lord will reign in eternity and beyond." And in the Psalm it is said: "But thou, O Lord, remainest for ever." Behold, O Mary, how great a Lord, how unfailing a Lord is He who is with thee! And because He is unfailingly with thee, therefore, thou also art unfailing with Him in eternity. For thou art that unfailing, that everlasting throne, the throne of the Son of God, of whom the Father saith by the Prophet: "His throne is like the sun in my sight, and like the moon perfect for ever and truly in eternity." Hence, we cannot only say with truth: "Thou, O Lord, endurest for ever," but we can also truly say: "Thou, O Lady, endurest for ever." What wonder if Mary, in her Son, remains forever, when even the benefits of Mary in her servants remain forever? For St. Bernard says: "In thee, O Mary, angels find joy, the just grace, sinners pardon forever." The Lord, therefore, is with thee, O never-failing Mary! Rejoice, O Mary, rejoice! Behold the most powerful Lord is with thee in such a manner that thou art most powerful with Him. The most wise Lord is with thee in such a way that thou art most wise with Him. The most rich Lord is with thee in such wise that thou art most rich with Him. The never-failing Lord is with thee in such wise that thou, together with Him, shalt never fail or be deficient.

Now, therefore, most powerful Lady, be a helper to us who are so impotent! Now, most wise Lady, be to us who are foolish a helper and a counsellor! O most wealthy Lady, be to us who are poor a benefactress! O most unfailing Lady, be to us feeble, failing creatures a perpetual support in every good deed!

CHAPTER IX

"THE LORD IS WITH THEE"

WE must now consider that this Lord, of whom it is said, "The Lord is with thee," is in a special manner the Lord of rational creatures, as man, the rational creature himself, says in the eighth Psalm: "O Lord, our Lord," etc. He is the Lord of all men; He is especially our Lord. As it is said in Isaias: "The Lord is our judge, the Lord is our lawgiver, the Lord is our king" (Is. XXXIII, 22.) The Lord is our lawgiver in this world; the Lord is our judge at the last judgment; the Lord is our King who will crown us in Heaven. This particular Lord of ours was with Mary in such a manner that He made her also our special Lady. Which St. Bernard acknowledged when he said: "Our Lady, our mediatrix, our advocate, reconcile us to thy Son, commend us to thy Son, present us before thy Son." But behold, this Lord of ours is a most loving, a most just, a most sure, a most renowned Lord. A Lord who was not loving in benefits, just in judgments, true in promises, nor renowned among his people, would not be thought much of. But Our Lord is most loving in liberality; most just in equity; most true in fidelity; most renowned in fame.

First, therefore, we must note that our own Lord, who is with Mary, is a most loving Lord in His infinite mercy. For He is the Lord of whom the Prophet saith: "Thou, Lord, art sweet and mild, and of much mercy to those who invoke Thee" (Ps. LXXXV, 5.) He is a Lord of much mercy in many temporal benefits, also in spiritual and eternal ones, which out of his great mercy He has bestowed upon us, and never ceases to bestow. Would that we were not ungrateful for so great mercies! Would that to such a merciful Lord we were very grateful as Isaias was, who said: "I will remember the tender mercies of the Lord, the praise of the Lord for all the things that the Lord hath bestowed upon us" (Is. LXIII, 7.) Behold, Mary, what a Lord He is, how loving, how merciful, the Lord who is with thee. And because this most merciful Lord is so merciful with thee, therefore thou art most merciful with Him, and truly of thee can it be said: "A throne shall be prepared in mercy, and one shall sit upon it in truth" (Is. XVI, 5.) The throne of divine mercy is Mary, the Mother of mercy, in whom all find the solace of mercy. For as we have a most merciful Lord, so have we a most merciful Lady. Our Lord is of much mercy to all who invoke Him, and our Lady is of much mercy to all who invoke her. Therefore St. Bernard excellently saith: "Let him be silent on the subject of thy mercy,

O blessed Virgin, who, having invoked it in his necessities, found it wanting." The Lord, therefore, is with thee, O most merciful Mary.

Secondly, note that our own special Lord, who is with Mary, is the most just Lord of equity, as it is well said in the Psalms: "The Lord is just and hath loved justices" (Ps. X, 8.) And again: "Thou art just, O Lord, and Thy judgment is right" (Ps. CXVIII, 137.) The Lord is most certainly just in all His judgments, in all causes, in all His deeds, as it is once more said in the Psalms: "The Lord is just in all His ways" (Ps. CXLIV, 17.) The Lord is so just in every path of justice that for no one will He depart from the way of justice. And therefore it is well said: "God will not except any man's person, neither will he stand in awe of any man's greatness, for He made the little and the great, and He hath equally care of all." Behold, O Mary, what kind of a Lord He is, what a just Lord, the Lord who is with thee! And because the Lord is most just with thee, therefore art thou most just together with Him. For thou art the rod of Aaron, straight, erect, flowering and fruitful; straight and erect, by justice and equity; flowering, by virginity; fruitful, by fecundity. For who would be the straight rod or stem, the upright rod or stem, if the rod of Aaron were not upright? What soul would be just, if Mary were not just? This is why St. Bernard says: "Who is just, if not the just Mary, from whom sprang the Sun of Justice?"

The Lord is, therefore, with thee, O most just Mary.

Thirdly, note that our own special Lord, who is with Mary, is most sure in fidelity and most faithful in surety, as the Prophet testifies, saying: "The Lord is faithful in all His ways." Think, therefore, upon those words of His, in which He has promised a crown to the just and hell to the wicked; and know that the faithful Lord will keep His words faithfully. He will faithfully do what He has spoken, as Ezechiel testifies: "I the Lord have spoken, and I will do" (Ezech. XXX, 12.) The most faithful Lord will most faithfully keep His words, as He Himself says in the Gospel: "Heaven and earth shall pass away," etc. Behold, O Mary, what kind of a Lord He is, what a faithful Lord He is, the Lord who is with thee! And because the most faithful Lord is faithfully with thee, therefore art thou most faithful together with Him. For thou art that most faithful dove of Noe, who hast most faithfully stood forth as mediatrix between the Most High God and the world submerged in a spiritual deluge. The crow was unfaithful, the dove most faithful. So also was Eve unfaithful; but Mary was found faithful. Eve was the unfaithful mediatrix of perdition; Mary was the faithful mediatrix of salvation. St. Bernard saith: "Mary was the faithful mediatrix, who prepared the antidote of salvation for both men and women." The Lord, therefore, is with thee, O most faithful Mary.

Fourthly, note that our special Lord, who is with

Mary, is the Lord who is most renowned for fame. He is of a great name, as St. Jerome testifies, saying: "There is none like to Thee, O Lord, and great art Thou, and great is Thy name" (Jerem. X, 6.) The name of the Lord is indeed of great fame and of great praise among all peoples, as the Royal Prophet testifies: "Kings of the earth, and all ye people, princes and all ye judges of the earth, young men and maidens, the old and the young, praise ye the name of the Lord!" (Ps. CXLVIII, 11–12.) The praise and fame of the name of God has extended not only to every people, but also to all time, as is manifest from the same Prophet who says: "May the name of the Lord be blessed from henceforth, now and forever." Likewise, the fame and praise of the name of the Lord has not only extended to every people and to all time, but also to every place, as the same Prophet says: "From the rising of the sun even to its setting, the name of the Lord is to be praised" (Ps. CXII, 2.) Behold, O Mary, how great a Lord, what a renowned Lord, is He who is with thee! And because He is a renowned and famous Lord, who is with thee in so renowned a manner, therefore art thou most renowned together with Him. For thou art well prefigured by Ruth, of whom it is written: "Be thou the example of virtue in Ephrata, and have a celebrated name in Bethlehem" (Ruth IV, 11.) O Mary of the most renowned name, how can thy name not be celebrated, which cannot even be devoutly uttered by anyone without some good coming to him? St. Bernard testifies to this, saying: "O great, O loving, O most praiseworthy Mary, thou canst not even be named, but thou enkindlest love; nor canst thou be thought of, without renewing the affection of those who love thee; thou canst never enter the portals of a loving memory without bringing with thee the sweetness which is divinely inseparable from thee." Mary, therefore, is well prefigured by that woman of renown, Judith, of whom it is written: "And she was greatly renowned among all, because she feared the Lord very much; neither was there any one that spoke an ill word of her" (Jud. VIII, 8.) Mary is indeed renowned because of her virtues and her praiseworthy example; but she is even more renowned because of her mercies and her unspeakable benefits, and more renowned still because of her graces and wonderful privileges. For what is more wonderful than to be a virgin mother, and the Mother of God? What wonder if Mary is renowned in the world from so many thousand benefits of her mercy, who is so renowned for that one benefit which she bestowed on man? St. Bernard says: "The renown of thy highest favour is that bestowed on the God-loving soul, who was reinstated by thee." The Lord is, therefore, with thee, O most renowned Mary. Rejoice, rejoice! Behold the most loving Lord is with thee in such a manner that thou also art most loving. The most just Lord is so with thee that thou, together with Him, art most just; the most renowned Lord is with thee in such a manner that thou also, together with Him, art most renowned. O most loving Mary, save us impious souls by thy merciful, loving kindness! O most just Mary, save us unjust souls by thy just equity! O most faithful Mary, save us perfidious souls by thy fidelity! O most renowned Mary, save us by thy sweet renown!

CHAPTER X

MARY THE DAUGHTER, MOTHER, SPOUSE, AND HANDMAID OF THE LORD

WE must now consider that this Lord, of whom it is said, "The Lord is with thee," is not alone in a general sense the Lord of every creature, not alone the Lord of the rational creature, but also in a most special sense the Lord of the virginal court of His most Holy Mother. Mary is singularly, both in body and in soul, the court of the Lord, the most holy house of God, of whom it is said in the Psalm: "Sanctity behooveth Thy house, O Lord." O singularly blessed House, who alone hast merited so singularly to have the Lord. St. Bernard saith: "Thou alone hast been found worthy that in thy virginal court the King of kings and the Lord of lords, coming from His royal throne, chose thee for His first dwelling among the sons of men." This singular Lord of Mary was with her in so special a way that He made her Lady, so that there never was one like her either before or after her. For she became in a wonderful and singular manner the daughter of the Lord, the mother of the Lord, the spouse of the Lord, and the handmaid of the Lord. If we wish to describe her relation to each Divine Person, we can say that the Lord who is with Mary is the Lord and Father, the Lord and Son, the Lord and Holy Ghost, the Lord who is triune and one. He is the Father and Lord, of whom Mary is the most noble daughter. He is the Son and Lord, of whom Mary is the most worthy Mother; He is the Holy Ghost and Lord, of whom Mary is the most just spouse; He is the Lord Triune and One, of whom Mary is the most submissive handmaid. Mary certainly is the Daughter of the Most High Eternity, the Mother of the Most High Truth, the Spouse of the Most High Goodness, the Handmaid of the Most High Trinity.

First, therefore, note, that this Lord, who is so singularly with Mary, is the Lord of whom Mary is the most noble daughter. Of this Lord and of this daughter can be understood that which Booz said: "Blessed art thou of the Lord, my daughter, and thy latter kindness has surpassed the former" (Ruth iii, 10.) Therefore Mary is the daughter blessed by the Lord; by the Most High Lord, I say, whose daughter she is. O truly noble daughter of the most noble King, who hast been so abundantly adorned interiorly with manifold glory, that truly it can be said of thee: "All the glory of the King's daughter is from within" (Ps. XLIV.) Therefore Mary, as the most true daughter of the King, was most abundantly drawn to the kingdom, as St. Bernard testifies, saying:

"Thou, a delicate daughter, and full of all grace, dearly beloved in thy delights, art drawn to the glory of thy beauty, and as a sign of love." This blessed daughter surpassed her former kindness by the latter; for great as the mercy of Mary was while she was still an exile in this world, much greater is her mercy now that she reigns in Heaven. Now by her innumerable benefits she shows men a greater mercy, for she now sees more clearly the untold miseries of mankind. For the splendour of her former mercy Mary was fair as the moon; but for the splendour of her latter mercy she resembles the sun. For as the sun surpasses the moon in the greatness of his splendour, so the latter mercy of Mary surpasses in greatness her former mercy. Who is there upon whom the sun and the moon do not shine? Who is there upon whom the mercy of Mary does not shine? Hear what St. Bernard thinks of this: "As the sun shines indifferently upon the good and the bad, so when Mary is petitioned, she does not discuss the merits of the petitioners, but shows herself ready to hear them, is most merciful to all, and in fine she compassionates the misery of all with most abundant affection." The Lord is with thee, therefore, O Mary, as a father with a most noble daughter.

Secondly, note that the Lord who is so singularly with Mary, is the Lord whose most worthy mother she is. Of this Lord and of this mother Elizabeth said: "Whence is this to me, that the mother of my

Lord should come to me?" The Mother of the Lord, the Virgin and Mother, is a most worthy mother. She is the Mother who is most becoming to such a Son. She is the Mother to whom such a Son is most becoming. She is the one, than whom God could make no greater. God could make a greater world, God could make a greater Heaven, but a greater mother than the Mother of God He could not make. St. Bernard saith: "No other mother was becoming to God than a virgin; nor was any other son becoming to a virgin than God." A greater among mothers than Mary and a greater among sons than Jesus could not be born. This mother is, therefore, the flower of mercy, the mother of the Sun of justice, the mother of the Fountain of wisdom, the mother of the King of glory. She is the mother of Him, I say, whose mercy leads us to love, whose justice to fear, whose wisdom to know, whose glory to hope. Mary is, therefore, the mother of Him who is in fact our love by mercy, our fear by justice, our knowledge by wisdom, our hope by glory, so that she can truly say: "I am the mother of fair love, and of fear, and of knowledge, and of holy hope" (Ecclus. XXIV, 24.) But is Mary the Mother of Christ only? Nay, what is most joyful, she is not only the Mother of Christ, but also the Mother of all the faithful. St. Ambrose saith: "If Christ is the brother of all believers, is not she, who brought forth Christ, the mother of all believers?" Oh, dearly beloved, let us all rejoice, and exclaim: "Blessed is the Brother, by whom Mary is our Mother; and blessed is the Mother, by whom Christ is our Brother." St. Anselm says: "Lady and Mother, by whom we have such a Brother, what thanks, what praise shall we pay to thee?" God is, therefore, with thee, O Mary, as a son with a most worthy mother.

Thirdly, note that this Lord who is so singularly with Mary is the Lord whose most beautiful spouse Mary is. To this Lord, as to this spouse, we can apply the word of Osee: "I will espouse thee to myself in justice, and in judgment, and in mercy, and in commiserations, and I will espouse thee to me in faith; and thou shalt know that I am the Lord" (Osee II, 19–20.) Behold a beautiful spouse, beautiful in justice, and in the judgment of her looks, beautiful in compassion and in mercy in the regard of her neighbours, and beautiful in faith in the sight of God. Beautiful indeed in the justice of her life, and in the judgment of her conscience, beautiful in mercy, in affection, and in compassion in her deeds. Beautiful in faith, whereby she believed all that was to be believed above herself, and whereby she believed all that was to be done in her, according to that word: "Blessed art thou who hast believed, because all shall be fulfilled in thee, which has been said to thee by the Lord" (Luke I, 45.) But behold Mary, the Spouse of the Holy Spirit, as she is and was most beautiful in conversation, so also is she most sweet in her address, as it is said in the Canticle of Canticles: "As a dropping honeycomb," etc. Oh, what honey-flowing words have those sweet lips of Mary often distilled! Had she not indeed milk and honey under her tongue in those two sweet words which she addressed to Gabriel? Had not Mary milk upon her tongue when she said: "How shall this be done, for I know not man?" (Luke I, 34.) Had she not honey on her tongue when she uttered that honey-sweet word: "Behold the handmaid of the Lord, be it done unto me according to thy word"? From the sweetness of this word, throughout the whole world, the Heavens have dropped honey. Mary had honey on her tongue in her eloquent words to God; she had milk on her tongue in her agreeable speech to her neighbour. Of how great sweetness and beauty is that Spouse of the Supreme Consoler! Because, as St. Augustine says, "Who is this virgin, so holy that the Holy Spirit deigns to come to her? So beautiful, that God chooses her for His Spouse?" The Lord is, therefore, with thee, O Mary, as a bridegroom with his beloved spouse.

Fourthly, note that this Lord, who is so singularly with Mary, is the Lord whose most devout handmaid she is, as she herself testifies: "Behold the handmaid of the Lord." Mary is the handmaid of God the Father, of God the Son, and of God the Holy Ghost. What wonder if she is the handmaid of that Lord, when her son is the servant of this Lord, according to the human nature assumed from His mother? He

Himself confesses it in the Psalm, where He says: "O Lord, because I am thy servant, and the son of thy handmaid." O what a good handmaid, and what a good son of the handmaid! Alas, how many are bad handmaids, and bad sons of the handmaids. But what saith the Scripture? "Cast out the bondwoman and her son." We read in Genesis of the handmaid of Sara that, seeing that she herself had conceived, she despised her mistress. Therefore, the evil handmaid Agar is puffed up by her fecundity; but the good handmaid Mary is made fecund by her humility. That proud handmaid despised her mistress; the Lord looked on this humble handmaid, as she herself says: "He hath regarded the humility of his handmaid." O Christian soul, handmaid of the Lord, with Mary cultivate fecundity in such a manner that you may not be wanting in humility; that, therefore, you may not be puffed up by your fecundity in good works, notice the humble handmaid, look upon the humble Mary. "Behold," she says, "the handmaid of the Lord." St. Ambrose says: "See her humility, see her devotion. She calls herself the handmaid of the Lord, she who is chosen to be His Mother; nor is she elated by the promise. O truly admirable humility! Behold in what manner Mary designs not only to be the handmaid of the Lord, but also the handmaid of the servants of the Lord. For it is she who is signified by Abigail, who sent messengers that she might be brought to David, saying: "Behold, let thy servant be a handmaid, that

Daughter, Mother, Spouse, Handmaid

she may wash the feet of the servants of my Lord" (1 Kings XXV, 41.) By the blessed handmaid Mary, how many servants of the Lord have been washed, how many faithful by her prayers have been cleansed from their sins! For she, as it were, offered water for their feet when she obtained for them tears of compunction for their sins. The Lord is with thee, therefore, O Mary, as with a most devout handmaid. The Father is with thee; the Son is with thee; the Holy Ghost is with thee. St. Bernard says: "The Father is with thee, because He made His Son thine; the Son is with thee, who, in order to work in thee an admirable secret, in a wonderful manner unlocked the secret room of generation, and kept for thee the seal of virginity; the Holy Spirit is with thee, who together with the Father sanctified thy womb. The Lord is, therefore, with thee," the Lord, whose daughter thou art, than whom none is more noble; the Lord, whose mother thou art, than whom none is more wonderful; the Lord, whose spouse thou art, than whom none is more lovable; the Lord, whose handmaid thou art, than whom none is more humble, nor ever was, nor ever will be. Therefore, O Lady, because so great a Lord is in such a manner and so much with thee, grant that by grace He may also be with us.

CHAPTER XI

MARY FOR HER OWN SAKE AND FOR OURS IS FITLY COMPARED TO THE AURORA

Dominus tecum—The Lord is with thee. That devout client of Mary, St. Anselm, alluding to these sweet words, says: "Mary, I beseech thee, by the grace by which the Lord wished so to be with thee, and thee with Him, grant for His sake, according to the same grace, His mercy to me; grant that the love of thee may be ever with me, and that my care may be about thee; grant that the cry of my necessity may be with thee, as long as it lasts, and that the look of thy loving kindness may be on me as long as I live; grant that my joy in thy beatitude may ever be with me, and that compassion for my misery may be with thee as far as it is expedient for me."

The Lord is with thee, O Mary. Certainly with thee, as the sun is with the aurora which goeth before him; with thee as the flower is with the stem which produces it; with thee, as the King is with the Queen going in to him. For the Sun, which is the most lightsome of all luminaries, the Flower which is more precious than all flowers, and the King, who is more glorious than all kings, is Our Lord Jesus Christ. The aurora, therefore, going before this Sun with resplendent radiance, the stem producing by a most wonderful flowering this Flower, the Queen entering in to the King in solemn procession, is the most Blessed Virgin Mary. Of all these points we shall treat in order.

The Lord is with thee. With thee, certainly, as the sun is with the aurora going before it, and preceding its rise, and beginning the day by its light. Truly, indeed, Mary, the aurora of the world, prepared in a most singular manner by the Eternal Sun, being thus marvellously irradiated, herself prepares the rising of this Sun, has wonderfully inaugurated for the world the day of grace of such a Sun, as St. Bernard says: "Like the aurora exceedingly resplendent hast thou come into the world, O Mary, when thou didst foreshew the splendour of the true Sun by such a wonderful radiance of sanctity that truly the day of salvation, the day of propitiation, the day which the Lord hath made, was worthy to be begun by thy bright light." Mary is, therefore, the aurora, of whom it is said: "Who is this, who cometh forth," etc. Fitly is she compared to the aurora, as well for herself, as for us; for herself especially, for us in general. Mary for herself is well compared to the aurora according to Scripture; first, because of the driving away of the night of sin; secondly, because of the approach of the light of grace; third, because of the rising of the Sun of justice; fourth, because of the place of her throne of glory. First, in her most full sanctification; secondly, in her most bright conversation; thirdly, in her most wonderful generation of her Son; fourthly, in her most glorious Assumption.

First, note that Mary is, as it were, a happy aurora because of the absence or happy driving away of guilt in her own sanctification. Therefore Job, cursing the night in which it was said: "A man is conceived," said: "Let the stars darken their light. Let it expect light and not see it, nor the rising of the dawning of the day" (Job III, 9.) What is meant here by the stars, by the light, by the dawn? I say that the stars are the souls of the Saints; the light is the Holy of holies; the dawn is the Queen of Saints. The stars indeed are all the Saints, who never abandon good order and discipline of morals, the course of fervour and of a good life, and so they fight with vigour against the devil. Of these stars it is well said in the Book of Judges: "The stars remaining in their order and courses fought against Sisara" (Judg. V, 20.) Sisara is interpreted, *taking away the departing one*, and it signifies the devil, who takes anyone that departs from God. The light signifies the Holy of Holies, Jesus Christ, as He Himself shows, saying: "I am the light of the world, who followeth Me, walketh not in darkness" (John VIII, 12.)

Let us, brethren, follow this light, lest, walking in

darkness, we should fall into the mire of sin and the pit of hell. Let us follow not haltingly, according to what is said, "How long will you halt between two sides? If the Lord is God, follow Him; but if Baal is, follow ye him" (3 Kings XVIII, 21.) The dawn, whose rising the night does not see, signifies the Blessed Virgin, whose nativity was not initiated by the night of original sin. For the night which Job cursed, the night in which man was conceived, is original sin; in which we are all conceived. Hence the Psalmist says: "In sins did my mother conceive me." Because all the Saints are conceived in sin, they are born in sin, and hence it is rightly said that this night has seen no light.

Secondly, note that Mary is, as it were, a happy aurora, because of her happy progress in the light of grace, according to that word: "Who is this that advances like the aurora," etc. (Cant. VI, 9.) For as the light of the aurora progresses by gradually growing in brightness, so Mary advanced by advancing in the splendour of grace and of a good life. She made progress indeed by advancing in all virtues universally, so that in all the glory of all virtue she was, as it were, in herself the rising aurora, fair as the moon to her neighbours, as the sun towards God. She made progress also by advancing in special virtues, of which St. Bernard speaks thus: "Charity burned in Mary by seeking grace, virginity was resplendent in her body, in service she was eminent in humility." By the glory of these virtues Mary was, as it were, the rising aurora in her shining virginity, fair as the moon in her resplendent humility, clear as the sun in her radiant charity. Happy he who cultivates these three splendours, these three virtues of Mary, by which she conceived the God and Master of all virtues, as St. Bernard again testifies, saying: "She who was already full of grace found grace, that, being fervent in charity, intact in virginity, devout in humility, she might become pregnant without any intercourse with man, and might bring forth a child without the usual travail."

Thirdly, note that Mary is, as it were, a happy aurora, because of the happy rising of the Sun of justice. For the Sun of justice, Christ Our Lord, by means of His aurora, Mary, rose upon this world. His rising was unaccompanied by any cloud of sin; wherefore this aurora was exceedingly resplendent in the rising of her Sun, according to that word: "As the light of the morning when the sun riseth, shineth in the morning without clouds" (2 Kings, XXIII, 4.) The light of this morning is the holiness of Mary, by which the Sun of justice, who was about to come forth from her, deigned to irradiate her. Of this St. Bernard well saith: "Rightly, O Mary, hast thou fulfilled the office of the morning. For the Sun of justice, who was Himself about to proceed from thee, preventing as it were His own birth by a certain morning splendour, copiously transfused thee with the rays of His own light." The light of this morning shone forth wonderfully when the Sun rose without clouds, that is, when Christ was born without any of the darkness of original sin. Behold, here it is said that the sun rose without clouds, and in Exodus we read that the bush was on fire without being burned; and in Daniel, that a stone was cut without hands. What, therefore, is signified by the sun, by the fire, by the stone, if not Christ? For He Himself is the sun enlightening the intellect, the fire enkindling the affections, the stone strengthening us against defect. I say that Jesus Christ is the sun illuminating the intellect, according to Malachias: "The sun of justice will rise upon you who fear my name" (IV, 2.) See, therefore, if thou fearest the Lord, for it is written: "Who feareth God, neglecteth nothing" (Ecclus. VII, 19.) Again Christ is the fire enkindling the affections, as the Apostle says to the Hebrews: "Our God is a consuming fire" (Hebr. XII, 29.) This fire was not only in the bush of the virginal womb, but also in the bush of her devout heart. They have felt this fire who said: "Were not our hearts burning within us," etc. Again, Christ is the stone strengthening us against failings, if we are well founded upon Him. Therefore it is said in St. Matthew: "The rains fell, and the floods came, and the winds blew, and they beat upon that house, and it fell not, for it was founded on a rock" (VII, 25.) Behold, neither the rain of heretical eloquence, nor the floods of worldly concupiscence, nor the winds of human violence, could injure the house of a mind founded upon the rock of Christ. What does it mean, therefore, that the sun rises without a cloud, the bush is on fire without being consumed, the stone is cut without hands, unless it be that Christ, who is the sun of truth, the fire of charity, the stone of firmness or of eternity, is conceived and born without the cloud of original sin, without the fire of carnal concupiscence, without the agency of the marital embrace? For in the conception of Christ you will find neither sin in the offspring, nor concupiscence in the mother, nor the embrace of a father. That this Virgin conceived so miraculously, He could effect who sent beforehand so many wonderful things prefiguring this miracle, as St. Augustine testifies, saying: "He who wrote on the tablets of stone without iron, made Mary with child of the Holy Ghost; and He who produced bread in the desert without ploughing, impregnated the virgin without corruption; and He who made the rod to bud without rain, made the daughter of David bring forth without seed."

Fourthly, note that Mary is, as it were, a happy aurora because of her place in glory; and according to this Job well says of the aurora: "Didst thou . . . shew the dawning of the day its place?" (Job XXXVIII, 12.) Now certainly, our aurora, Mary, elevated high in Heaven, holds the place nearest to the Eternal Sun. We may consider that the throne of Mary in Heaven has a threefold greatness. The first is that she received Our Lord spiritually; the second, that she received Him corporeally; the third, that she received Him eternally. Behold the threefold place of Mary. I say that the first place in which Mary received Our Lord spiritually, is her mind, tranquil and peaceful, according to the Psalmist: "His place is in peace, and His dwelling in Sion," which, interpreted, means a mirror or contemplation. Whoever wishes to contemplate God, or to behold Him with the eyes of the mind, must make Him a place in peace in his mind; for without peace of mind no one can arrive at the knowledge of contemplation. Therefore the Apostle saith: "Follow peace with all men, and holiness, without which no man shall see God" (Hebr. XII, 14.) Oh, who shall relate, or who can even imagine, in what contemplations daily that Sion, that holy mind of Mary, was employed, while she fervently revolved in her mind all those mysteries known to herself above all mortals? Of this St. Jerome well says: "If there are in you any bowels of piety or mercy, consider with what love was crucified, with what desire this virgin burned, while she revolved in her soul all that she had heard and seen, all that she had known; with what emotions she was moved, being filled with the Holy Ghost, with the thrilling knowledge of heavenly secrets." The place in which Mary conceived corporeally was her holy womb, to which may be applied the word of Genesis: "The river which came forth from the paradise of pleasure [Jesus Christ from the Virgin's womb] was to water the garden" (Gen. II, 10.) The special paradise is Mary; the universal paradise is the Church. Happy is the watering of both these gardens by the mystic river from the womb of Mary, Jesus Christ, who has said: "I will water my garden of plants" (Ecclus. XXIV, 42.) Well, therefore, doth St. Jerome say, commenting on these words: "I saw her coming up beautiful from the banks of the water." Well is it said, "above the rivers of water," because the Lord had nourished her on the waters of refreshment, and brought her up on them; from whom many rivers emerge, water all the land of delights, and flow over the garden of pleasure." Again, the place wherein Mary received the Lord when she was about to dwell forever in Heaven is the place of glory, of which the Lord said to Job: "Hast thou shown the dawn its place?" (XXXVIII, 12), as if he said, "Not thou, but I." It does not belong to thee to show Mary, the dawn, her place in Heaven, but to me. Well doth he say, *her place,* as it were appropriating it to her, and discriminating it from all the other places of the Saints. Hence we read: "The priests brought in the ark of the covenant into its place" (3 Kings, VIII, 6.) This place is most certainly above all the choirs of angels. Finally, this place is the most worthy in Heaven, as St. Bernard testifies saying: "Neither was there in the world a more worthy place than the bridal chamber of the virginal womb, in which Mary received the Son of God, nor in the heavens one more worthy than the royal throne to which the Son of Mary raised her." Mary is compared to the dawn; first, because she put an end to the night of guilt, in her most full holiness; secondly, because of the advance of the light of grace in her most bright conversation; thirdly, because of the bringing forth of the Sun of justice in her wonderful generation of her Son; fourthly, because of her taking possession of her place in glory in her most glorious Assumption.

Then we have to consider that the most lightsome Virgin is compared to the aurora, not alone for herself, but also because of us. For as in Scripture she is signified by the aurora, she is for us a mediatrix with God, with the angels a peace-maker, against the devils a defender, to ourselves a light-giver.

First note that our aurora, Mary, is for us a mediatrix with God, as is signified in the Psalm: "Thine is the day and thine is the night, thou hast made the aurora and the sun" (Ps. LXXIII, 6.)

Thus St. Gregory well says: "The day is the life of the just, but the night is taken to mean the life of the sinner." And therefore the Lord went before the children of Israel by night in a pillar of fire, by day in a pillar of cloud, and because the cloud protected the wicked from the fire of His wrath, and He burns the wicked like fire. Therefore the sun signifies Christ, who enlightens the elect and burns the reprobate. He sometimes burns them severely in this world, but more severely at the last judgment, and most severely of all in hell. Of this threefold burning can be understood that word of Ecclesiasticus: "The sun three times as much, burneth the mountains" (Ecclus. XLIII, 4), that is, proud sinners. On this account we are in need of a refreshment, of a mediatrix between us and the just Sun. And well, therefore, doth the Psalmist, in the aforesaid verse, place the aurora midway between the night and the sun, because in the natural order it certainly holds this place. The aurora, therefore, is the Blessed Virgin Mary, who is the most excellent mediatrix between the night and the sun, between man and God, between unjust man and just God; she is the best cooler of the wrath of God. St. Bernard bears witness, saying: "Man now has secure access to God, for he has as a Mediator of his cause the Son before the Father and the Son before the Mother. The Son shows His naked body, with His wounds in hands, feet, and side to His Father; Mary shows her breasts to her Son. There can be no question of a repulse, where so many marks of charity appear in one, and present their prayer."

Secondly, note that our aurora, Mary, is for us a peace-maker with the angels, as it is signified in

Genesis, where we read that the angel who wrestled with Jacob blessed him at dawn. For when the angel said, "Let me go, it is morning," Jacob would not let him go till he had blessed him. In the morning took place the struggle between the angel and Jacob, the discord between God, the angels, and men. For man by sin had offended his Creator; and the Creator being offended, every creature was offended; how much more she who is more closely bound to the Creator! This struggle, therefore, was perhaps a figure of that discord. But when the aurora appeared at the coming of Mary, men and angels were pacified, because in that dawn, in the Virgin Mary herself, man received the angelic benediction. For the angel said to the Virgin: "Blessed art thou among women," and by this blessing of the Virgin man obtains the blessing of peace and salvation in the Virgin's Son —that blessing of which the Apostle says: "Blessed be the God and Father of our Lord Jesus Christ, who hath blessed us in every blessing in the heavenly places in Christ," which blessing the Son Himself will confirm when He will say: "Come, ye blessed of My Father," etc. As Jacob gave thanks at the rising of dawn, let us, therefore, thank Mary for that blessing by which we made peace with the angel. By the aurora, by the dawn, by Mary, men made peace with the angels, since the time when, by Mary, the depleted choirs of angels were peopled by men, as St. Anselm signifies, saying: "O wonderfully singular and singularly wonderful Woman, by whom the elements are renewed, the injuries of hell repaired, men are saved, angels are restored!"

Thirdly, note that Mary, our dawn, is for us a defender against the devils, as signified in Job, where it is said of the murderer, the thief, and the adulterer, "He diggeth through houses in the dark, as in the day they had appointed for themselves, and they have not known the light" (Job XXIV, 16.) "If the morning suddenly appear, it is to them the shadow of death" (Job XXIV, 17.) The murderer is a devil, the thief is a devil, the adulterer is a devil. The murderer, because he takes human life; the thief, because, whatever good thing he can rob us of, he does; the adulterer, because he corrupts the soul, which is the spouse of God. Alas, what evil these wicked people do us, what evil the wicked spirits do us! For sometimes they dig in the darkness of ignorance, in the darkness of obscurity, the interior houses of our minds, the houses indeed, of which it is said in the Psalm: "God is known in their houses" (Ps. XLVI, 14.) Without doubt they dig into our souls by their piercing temptations, those houses in which He joyfully dwells who has said: "To-day I must abide in thy house" (Luke XIX, 5.) And having dug through these houses, having indeed dug into the minds of men through to an unhappy consent to sin, alas, how great evils these wicked ones do in souls by murder, theft, and adultery! That we may evade such perils, let the dawn come, let Mary help us! For if the morning shall suddenly appear, if she quickly comes to our aid, and if her grace and mercy supervene, it will be as the shadow of death to the demons; they will tremble and fly; they will fear, as men fear and fly the shadow of death. Well doth St. Bernard say: "An army of enemies does not so much fear an immense host of armed soldiers, as the powers of the air do the very name of Mary, and her holy example; they fly and melt like wax before a fire, wherever they find the frequent invocation of this holy name, its remembrance and imitation."

Fourthly, note that Mary, our dawn, is, as regards ourselves, a light-giver to help us to do good. For from the first rays of light, workmen begin to work. Whence in the second book of Esdras it is said: "And let us do the work; and let one-half of us hold the spears from the rising of the morning, till the stars appear" (2 Esdras 21.) Two things are needful to us, namely, that we be earnest in our good works, and therefore well do the builders say: "Let us do the work." What work is this, but that of which the Apostle says: "While we have time, let us do good to all, especially to those who are of the household of the faith" (Gal. VI, 10.) Well do they say: Let *us* do the work, not our representatives. And in another passage: In all things let us show ourselves as the ministers of God. But Mary did not commission a nurse, or a representative, but showed herself always a handmaid to the Lord, as St. Augustine testifies: "Mary without doubt was a worker, who bore Him in her womb, and when He was brought forth, nourished and nursed Him, laid Him in the manger, and during the whole of His infancy served Him as a loving Mother, so that even to the death of the cross she never left Him." Not only did she follow Him by her footsteps, as from the love of a son, but also by the imitation of His life, as out of reverence for a Lord." It is needful for us, not only to be instant in good works, but also to resist vices; and therefore well do they add that the lances should be held; for we should hold the lance of zeal against the attacks of vice, against the attacks of the devil, the flesh, and the world. Of these lances it is well said in Jeremias: "Furbish the spears, put on the coats of mail." By the coat of mail of justice we are protected, but with the lance or spear of zeal we attack evil. If thou dost not launch the spear of zeal in this world against evil, God will use the lance of His zeal against thee on judgment day. Therefore it is said in the Book of Wisdom: "He will sharpen His dire wrath as a spear" (Wisd. V, 21.) Oh, what a warrior was Mary, whose holy zeal was her spear. St. Bernard says to her: "Thou wert a formidable warrior, for thou wert the first manfully to attack him who had supplanted the first Eve." Therefore, that we may faithfully persist in good works and manfully resist vices, it is needful for us to look on the example of Mary, to implore the suffrages of Mary. Then, as it were from the rising of the morning, we work, when being irradiated by the example and the life of Mary, when being illuminated by the patronage and the mercy of Mary, we are incited to good. We ought to work well till the rising of the stars, that is, until our souls, having become lightsome like stars, go forth from our bodies and fly to the stars. But above every star that ever appeared, above every star that ever will come forth in the heavens, the most splendid is Mary, our aurora, our morning, as St. Bernard testifies, saying: "Thou art the most vivid image of the true Sun, amongst the myriads of stars that are before God, thou shinest forth gloriously in Heaven by thy virginal purity." Thus you see how fittingly Mary is called the morning, the aurora. The Lord is with thee, O Mary, as the sun is with the dawn. Therefore, O Lady, most sweet morning, our Lady, most sweet Mary, let us be with the Sun of Justice, our Lord Jesus Christ, thy Son, who with the Father and the Holy Ghost liveth and reigneth for ever and ever. Amen.

CHAPTER XII

MARY A ROD OR STEM, AND A FLOWERING STEM

The Lord is with thee. Having seen how the Lord was with Mary, as the sun is with the dawn which goes before it, let us now see how the Lord is with Mary as the flower is with the budding stem. For Mary is that rod of which it is said in Isaias: "There shall come forth a rod from the root of Jesse, and a flower shall ascend from that root, and the Spirit of the Lord shall rest upon Him, the spirit of wisdom and of understanding, the spirit of counsel and of fortitude, the spirit of knowledge and of piety, and He shall be filled with the spirit of the fear of the Lord" (Is. XI.) Let us place these words before the eye of our mind, and direct our consideration first to the rod and then to the flower.

First consider, that this rod, this royal rod, is the Virgin Mary, as St. Ambrose testifies, saying in speaking to the Blessed Virgin: "Thou thyself, who hast brought forth the Lord, art of the land of Israel; thou hast grown into a rod, the rod from the root of Jesse; thou hast arisen and flowered, O rod of Aaron; thou hast flowered and brought forth."

For Mary is a rod smoking with incense, a rod of wood, a rod of gold, a rod of iron. Mary is a rod smoking to beginners, a rod of wood to those who are advancing, a rod of gold to the perfect, a rod of iron to the incorrigible and the demons.

I say that the Virgin Mary is as a smoking rod to beginners and to penitents. Of this rod it is said in the Canticle of Canticles: "Who is she that cometh up from the desert, as a pillar of smoke of aromatical spices, of myrrh, and frankincense, and of all the powders of the perfumer?" (Cant. III, 6.) The desert is the heart of the sinner, which is indeed devoid of grace and virtue. The aromatical spice, the sweet incense of the soul, is the aspiration of hope for pardon. The Blessed Virgin Mary, therefore, came up from the desert as a pillar of smoke, when, by her prayers, the heart of the sinner received the smoking incense of pardon. This smoke is generated from the aromatical myrrh of contrition, and of incense in confession, and from all the powders of the perfumer in manifold satisfactions. No desert doth the Virgin Mary abhor, no sinner doth she despise; but wherever she passes, she spreads the sweet incense of pardon. Excellently, therefore, does St. Bernard say: "Thou dost not abhor or despise any sinner, however foul, if he but sighs to thee, and begs with a repentant heart for thy pardon; thou drawest him from the abyss of despair with thy loving hand, thou breathest upon him the remedy of hope, and embracest him, the outcast of all the world, with maternal affection, thou cherishest him and dost not desert him, until he is reconciled with the tremendous Judge."

Again, Mary is the rod of wood, the rod which is flowering to those who are advancing. Of this rod it is said in the Book of Wisdom that the rod of Aaron, which was of wood, bore fruit and flowers. By the flowers are signified virtues, which, after the passing of the devilish winter, rise up in hearts, as it is well said in the Canticle: "Now the winter is over and gone, and flowers have appeared in our land." Let the winter, therefore pass, let that torpor in which charity grows cold, pass, and then the flowers of virtue will appear again. Oh, with what flowers the flowering Virgin hath abounded, as St. Bernard says, speaking to her: "Thou art as a garden-plot of holy perfumes, planted by the heavenly Perfumer, delectably flourishing with the flowers of all virtues." As flowers signify virtues, so fruits denote the works of the virtues. Of these it is well said: "By their fruits you shall know them." When, therefore, we advance in virtues and in the works of the virtues, we advance by the examples and merits of Mary, and then the Virgin Mary is to us a rod of wood, flowering and fruitful.

Likewise the Virgin Mary is to the perfect and contemplative a golden rod. We read that Esther with two maidens went to King Assuerus, and when she had become faint from exceeding fear, the King held out to her the golden sceptre to console her. Esther means "raised up" or "hidden," and is a figure of the contemplative soul, whom God raises up in contemplation and hides in the hidden place of His face from the tumult of men. This soul by contemplation enters into Christ the King. The two maidens by whose help she enters are the two powers of the soul, the intellect, which proceeds by way of knowledge, and the affections, which follow by love. The soul which has thus entered into Christ, sometimes faints away by a kind of stupor, when she recognises the inaccessible brightness of the divine glory, or the terrible severity of the divine justice. The golden rod, the royal sceptre, is the Virgin Mary. Golden indeed by her charity, royal by her nobility; golden by her purity, royal by her justice; golden by her incorruption and virginal integrity, royal by her domination and power. This is the happy rod, which is extended with clemency to comfort the contemplative soul, when the happy Virgin Mary, by contemplation and devotion of this soul, which is so loving and sweet, enters into it; so that from this the soul is strengthened against fear of the divine splendour and justice. The contemplative soul of St. Anselm desired this rod to be extended to it, when he exclaimed: "O Virgin fair to look upon, lovable to contemplate, delightful to love, who transcendest the capacity of the heart, give thyself, O Lady, to the weak soul who followeth thee."

Likewise the Virgin Mary is as an iron rod to the demons and incorrigible sinners. To this rod we may apply that word of the Psalm: "Thou shalt rule them with a rod of iron." O Mary, rod of gold to the perfect, rod of gold to the hard, rod of gold to men, rod of iron and hard to the demons, keep the demons from us! This, Lady, we ask, and we ask it devoutly with Innocent: "Hail, loving Mother of God, who from the dignity by which thou art Mother of God, hast power to restrain the demons, restrain the demons lest they hurt us; command the angels to guard us." Thus, therefore, the Blessed Virgin Mary is to us a rod of smoke or incense in our conversion, a flowering rod in our lives, a golden rod in our contemplation, an iron rod in our defence. St. Bernard, admiring and worthily contemplating this rod, saith: "O Virgin, sublime rod, to how great a height thou raisest thy summit—even unto Him who sitteth on the throne, unto the Lord of Majesty, for thou castest deep down thy roots in humility."

Let us now consider the flower of this rod; let us consider in the royal rod, and in the Virgin Mary a fourfold flower, a precious flower, a flower of virginity, of virtuous reputation, of miraculous fecundity, and of glorious immortality.

Of this flower consider, first, in Mary the flower

of precious virginity, which is virginity itself. Of this it is said in Isaias: "The desert shall rejoice and shall flower as a lily." Mary can fittingly be said to be a desert, who was so willing to be alone, who was in her voluntary solitude visited by an angel. Therefore St. Ambrose well says: "Alone in the inner part of her house, she whom no man could see, he found her alone without a companion, alone without a witness." In what manner this desert, the Virgin Mary, should rejoice, let her say herself: "And my spirit hath rejoiced in God my Saviour." This desert of earth flowered like a lily by virginity. O angelical lily! O heavenly flower! O truly heavenly flower! whom that supercelestial Bee hath so loved. For St. Bernard saith: "That Bee who feedeth among the lilies, who dwelt in a flowering fatherland, when He flew to Nazareth, which is interpreted a flower, flew towards thee, and came to the sweet smelling flower of thy perpetual virginity, he rested upon it, he embraced it." The flower of virginity has as many petals, so to speak, as the conditions and praises of virginity. Oh, how greatly the crowns of this flower were multiplied by Mary! St. Ambrose says: "In the whole world the flower Mary weaves unfading crowns, and keeps the royal court of purity with immaculate affection, until integrity perseveres to the palm of victory, that in maidens it may grasp the trophy of sanctity, and in the footprints of the Virgin Mary, attain to the heavenly bridal chamber."

Secondly, consider in Mary the flower of virtuous reputation, of manners and of life, and hear what she herself says: "My flowers are the fruits of honour and riches" (Ecclus. XXIV, 23.) Of these it is also said: "Our bed is flowering." Behold, we find flowers in the earth, and in the bed. The earth is the mind of the active (souls); the bed is the mind of contemplatives. The earth, I say, is the mind bearing fruit in good actions; but the bed is the mind seeking quiet in contemplation. Let the mind be active, or let it be contemplative, it should always be beautiful with flowers. Note also that the flower of honesty, of a good reputation, yea, the flower of any virtue has, as it were, as many petals as it has good and meritorious works to show. Oh, how flowering was that earth, how flowering was the bed of Mary, who in the flowering virtue of her life flourished in the beauty of every virtue, as St. Bernard testifies, saying: "Thou art the casket of holy perfumes, O Mary, gathered by the heavenly Perfumer, delightfully blooming with the beautiful flowers of every virtue, among which three are excellent above all, the violet of humility, the lily of chastity, and the rose of charity."

Thirdly, consider in Mary the flower of her miraculous fecundity. This flower is the Son of the Virgin, of whom it is said: "There shall come forth a rod from the root of Jesse, and a flower shall arise from its root." Oh, how beautifully this flower came forth, being born without sin, and how sadly was it crushed by dying, as it were like a sinner, according to that word: "Like a flower he goeth forth and is crushed." Oh, how white in His going forth, and how ruddy in His bruising was this flower! A flower, I say, delightful to the angels and most useful to men for life. St. Bernard saith: "The flower is the Son of the Virgin, a flower white and ruddy, a flower on whom the angels long to look, a flower by whose perfume mortals live again." Happy the wood which produces such a flower! Happier the stem or rod which in the wood produces this flower! Happy above all the flower, without whom there can neither be wood nor rod happy! Truly a most happy flower, in which the Holy Ghost so rested that without Him no one could have the grace of the Spirit. St. Jerome testifies to this, saying: "The Holy Ghost, who in the vast wood of the human race had found no rest, at last rested upon this flower, so that without Christ no one could be wise, no one could have understanding, or counsel, or fortitude, or learning, or piety, or the fear of the Lord." This flower has, as it were, as many petals as it had ministries and examples. If thou desirest to have this flower, thou must bend its stem down to thee by prayer. If the flower is exceedingly high by its divinity, the stem is flexible by its love. And if the flower is most rare, because neither in Heaven nor on earth is there found another one, it is nevertheless most common, like a flower not enclosed in a garden, but in a field exposed to all passersby. Therefore, well could Christ say: "I am the flower of the field." He can be called a flower of the field, not only because it is openly exposed to the view of all, but also because it is produced without human culture. This St. Bernard hath in mind when he says: "The field flourishes without any human aid, it is not sowed by anyone, not harrowed by the plough, not made fertile with manure; thus indeed did the womb of the Virgin flower, so did the chaste and entire interior of Mary like pastures of eternal greenness produce Him whose beauty sees not corruption, whose glory will never fade."

Fourthly, consider the flower of gracious immortality, of which it is said in Numbers that the rod of Aaron bore at the same time both flowers and fruit. The rod of Aaron prefigures the Virgin Mary. In the straightness of the rod is prefigured the integrity of Mary; in the flower, the beauty of her glorified body; and in the fruit, the beatitude of her soul. It is to be noted that in youth the body is most beautiful, as it is said: "In the morning it blooms and fades." But the flower perishes in death, as it is said in Isaias: "The grass is withered, and the flower is fallen." It will flower again in a glorious resurrection, according to the Psalmist: "My flesh has flowered again." This flower of the glorification of the body has, as it were, as many petals as the glorified body has gifts and rewards. And certainly the holy Doctors seem to hold it as probable, and strive with some show of reason to prove, and the pious sense of the faithful always held, that the Blessed Virgin was taken up body and soul into Heaven, and that her body and soul are now in glory. St. Augustine says: "I hold that Mary is in Christ and with Christ; in Christ, because in Him we live and move and have our being; with Christ, because she is assumed into glory." Therefore we worthily believe that Mary rejoices with ineffable joy both in body and soul, in her own Son, by her own Son; nor has she ever felt the sting of corruption because no stain was communicated to her integrity in bringing forth her Son, because she begot Him who is the whole and perfect life of all; let her be with Him, whom she bore in her womb; let her be with Him, who bore Him, nursed Him, and fed Him. Mary is the Mother of God, the servant of God, the nurse of God, the follower of God. According to this belief she can now say: "My flesh hath flowered again." And according to this she has at the same time both fruit and flowers: as flower, her glorified body; and for fruit, her glorified spirit. A flower indeed in the beauty of her glorious body; and fruit in the unspeakable pleasure of her soul. We must note that, according to the aforesaid fourfold flower, the Virgin Mary has a fourfold flower of virginity, and a fourfold flower of fecundity; she has the flower of good repute and the flower of humility; she has at the same time in her Child the flower of humanity and the fruit of the divinity; she has at the same time the flower of immortality in the body and the fruit of blessed pleasure in the soul. Let us, therefore, discern these flowers in the virginal rod, and gather these new flowers of joy from the virginal garden, which St. Bernard saw gathered and commended to us, when, speaking to Mary, he said: "Thy most holy womb, O Mary, is to us a garden of delights; because from it we gather the flowers of manifold joys as often as we think in our minds how great a sweetness flowed thence over the entire world." Therefore, most sweet Virgin Mary, behold, the Lord is truly with thee, as the flower is with the stem which produced it. Grant that the Lord may also be with me, yea, with all of us, and give to us this flower, the Lord Jesus Christ. Amen.

CHAPTER XIII

MARY COMPARED TO A QUEEN ENTERING INTO THE PALACE WITH THE KING

The Lord is with thee, O Lady most dear to the Lord, most intimate with the Lord! The Lord is with thee, O most well-fitted Lady, most worthy of the Lord! The Lord is with thee: with thee most certainly, according to what has been said above, as the sun is with the dawn which precedes it, as the flower is with the stem which produces it, as the king is with the queen entering into his palace.

Having seen how Mary is as the dawn to the eternal Sun, preventing the Sun of justice; having seen also how Mary is as the stem or rod to the eternal flower, producing the flower of mercy; let us now consider in what manner Mary is the Queen of the Eternal King, entering into glory.

Mary is that Queen entering in, of whom it is said that the queen entered into Jerusalem with a great company and with riches (3 Kings, X, 1.) Truly Mary is a queen. St. Augustine says: "We truly confess her to be the Queen of Heaven, because she brought forth the King of angels." I have spoken of this Queen in my sermon, "The Queen stood, etc."; therefore, I will now speak of her entrance.

We are to consider, therefore, that we find Mary going in, going forth, going on, and going above. Her going forth was of nature, her progress was of grace, her entrance was into glory, her elevation was in abundance.

She went forth by being born, she progressed by advancing in grace and virtue, she entered in by attaining, she surpassed all by her sanctity. She went forth without sin, she made progress beyond all example, she entered in without obstacle, she surpassed all without limits.

First consider that we find Mary going forth into the world by her nativity without sin. . . .

Secondly, consider that we find Mary advancing without equal by her grace. Therefore it is said in the Canticle: "Who is she that cometh forth as the rising dawn, fair as the moon, bright as the sun?" (Cant. VI, 9.) To these three luminaries, that is, the dawn, the moon, and the sun, Mary is fitly compared, for three excellent perfections shine forth in her. Resplendent virginity was in her mind and heart in a superlative degree; in her virginity shone forth fecundity, and in her fecundity shone forth a singular pre-eminence. A refreshing dawn and one pleasing to the birds was Mary; for by her virginity she cooled the ardour of the flesh, as St. Bernard says, speaking to her: "By the virtue of chastity thou didst extinguish in thy virginal flesh the ardour of the forbidden concupiscence, that He, in whose sight even the stars are not pure, judged thy flesh to be of such purity that He deigned to unite it to His own divine purity." She also by her virginity was pleasing to the birds of heaven, that is, to the angels of God, for, as St. Jerome says: "Virginity is always related to the angels." Therefore we read that the angel blessed Jacob in the dawn. Jacob may here signify a chaste spirit, because Jacob supplanted his brother, that is, the body, his body. He was blessed not only by the angel, but also by his father, in the dawn, or in the morning, that is, in the chaste Virgin Mary, to whom the angel said: "Blessed art thou among women." Likewise Mary was fair as the moon in the light-giving fecundity of her virginity; for the beauty of the moon consists in the light it receives from the sun. Think, therefore, what a beautiful moon was Mary, when that Eternal Sun was wholly received and conceived in her. Mary, therefore, is that moon in whose fulness that Man returned to the Church of whom it is said: "In the day of the full moon he will return to his house" (Prov. VII, 20.) The Blessed Virgin was the full moon, when it was said to her: "Hail, full of grace!" Again Mary was chosen as the sun in the illumining privilege of her fecundity, when not mere man alone, nor a real angel, but the Son of God Himself placed in her His tabernacle, when He was conceived in Mary. Without doubt it would have been most singular if the Virgin had conceived a mere man; but it would have been much more singular if the Virgin had conceived an angel. It was singular above all that a virgin conceived and brought forth God. Well, therefore, doth St. Augustine say: "Rightly is the Blessed Mary extolled by us with extraordinary praise, who has shown to the world so extraordinary a benefit, when she is raised to so sublime a height that, while the Word was from the beginning abiding with God, she should yet receive Him into her bosom from the highest heavens." The Blessed Virgin Mary, therefore, has advanced like the rising morning, in admirable virginity of mind and body; bright as the sun, in the adorable divinity of her virginal offspring.

Thirdly, consider that we find Mary entering into the glory of Heaven without obstacle. For what could have opposed such a great queen advancing with so great a retinue? She was prefigured by the Queen of Saba, of whom it is said: "Entering into Jerusalem with a great train, and riches, and camels that carried spices, and an immense quantity of gold and precious stones" (3 Kings X, 2.) Consider in these words the glory of Mary entering into the heavenly Jerusalem. Consider, I say, the excellence of her who enters, her power and her wealth. Consider the excellence of the primacy of our Queen Mary, insomuch as she is compared to the Queen of Saba, which signifies a cry. For Mary is the Queen of the world, where there is a cry of mourning. She is also the Queen of Heaven, where there is a cry of joy. For the dwellers in Heaven cry out, as it is said in the Apocalypse: "Holy, holy, holy, Lord God Almighty!" And this Queen of those who cry out, ceases not herself to cry out with the others, as St. Augustine says: "Thou, O Mary, fellow-citizen of the inhabitants of Heaven, being endlessly associated with the angels and archangels, ceasest not to cry out with untiring voice: "Holy, holy, holy!" She indeed is the queen whom the Psalmist describes, saying: "The queen stood on thy right hand, in gilded clothing, surrounded with variety" (Ps. XLIV, 10.) All can follow this Queen with confidence into the kingdom who have faithfully served her in this world. St. Bernard says: "Our Queen has gone before us: she has gone before us and has been so gloriously received that her servants may confidently cry out: 'Draw me after thee.'" Likewise consider in the entering in of our Queen the power of the retinue accompanying her, for it says: "with a multitudinous retinue." Mary entered into the heavenly Jerusalem with a multitudinous retinue of angelic powers. St. Jerome says: "We read how the angels have come to the death and burial of some of the Saints, and how they have accompanied the souls of the elect to Heaven with hymns and praises." And he adds: "How much more should we believe that the heavenly army, with all its bands, came forth rejoicing in festive array, to meet the Mother of God, surrounded her with effulgent light, and led her with praises and canticles to the throne prepared for her from the beginning of the world."

Likewise, consider in Mary the wealth of her merits, as it were in a dower of precious gifts: for she brought with her infinite gold in her love of God and of her neighbour, the precious gems of virtues and gifts, the spices of good works and examples. What I say of the treasures of Mary is little compared with what St. Bernard says. "In thy hands," he says, speaking to Mary, "are all the treasures of the mercies of the Lord. God forbid that thy hand should cease to give; for thy glory is not diminished, but augmented, when sinners are pardoned and the justified are taken up into glory." The Mother of God, therefore, entered into glory, as the Queen of Heaven, accompanied by a vast retinue of angels, with innumerable riches of merit.

Fourthly, consider that we find her surpassing all the Saints in the superabundance of her merits and rewards without end, according to the saying: "Many daughters have gathered together riches, thou hast surpassed them all." Thou hast indeed surpassed them in nature, in grace, in glory; thou hast surpassed all the daughters of men, all souls, all angelical intelligences, O Mary. I say that Mary in nature has surpassed all the daughters of men, for what nature does not admit of, she, a virgin, conceived, and brought forth, according to that word: "Behold a virgin shall conceive and bring forth a son." And it was not this alone that is above all nature, that a virgin should bring forth a son, but that she should bring forth God. Therefore, St. Jerome says: "What nature does not possess, what custom wots not, what reason knows nothing of, what the human mind cannot grasp, what the heavens fear, what the earth is astonished at, all this was what was divinely announced by the Angel Gabriel to Mary, and was fulfilled in Christ." Likewise, Mary surpassed in grace all the souls of the Saints, for she was not only full of grace, but overfull (*superplena*), as Gabriel signified, who said at first, "full of grace," and afterwards added: "And the Holy Ghost shall come upon thee." If, therefore, she was full of grace, whatever the Holy Spirit brought her afterwards was more than full measure; she was then more than full, she was surpassingly full (*superplena*). St. Bernard says: "While the Holy Spirit was coming, she was full of grace for herself (*plena sibi*); but when the Holy Spirit had come upon her, she was overfull and overflowed with grace for our sakes (*superplena nobis*)." So Mary surpassed in glory all the angelical intelligences; for she is the sapphire throne which, as we read in Ezechiel, is raised above the angelic firmament. St. Bernard says: "Mary ascended above every heavenly creature; up to the angels and even above these." So, therefore, Mary went forth, and advanced, and entered in, and went beyond all. She went forth, I say, by coming into this mortal life; she advanced in grace and privileges; she entered in by attaining to the Heavenly Kingdom; she surpassed all by exceeding the glory of all the blessed. Behold, therefore, O most sweet Virgin Mary, the Lord is truly with thee, as the sun is with the dawn which goes before it, as the flower is with the flowering stem, as the King is with the Queen entering in. O most sweet aurora, grant that the Sun of justice may also be with us! O most sublime Rod, grant that with us also may be the Flower of grace! O most powerful Queen, grant that the King of glory, Our Lord Jesus Christ, may stay with us!

CHAPTER XIV

MARY IS BLESSED ON ACCOUNT OF HER FULNESS OF GRACE, THE MAJESTY OF HER OFFSPRING, THE MULTITUDE OF HER MERCIES, THE GREATNESS OF HER GLORY

Blessed art thou among women. It has been shown how Mary, because of the innocence of her life, is saluted by the *Ave:* it has also been shown how she is rightly called "full of grace," because of the most copious affluence of her grace; it has moreover been shown how, because of the special presence of Our Lord with her, she is saluted with the words "The Lord is with thee." Now we have to show how, because of the most pleasing reverence of her person, she is hailed as *"Blessed among women."* Behold, therefore, that the Archangel Gabriel by saluting the glorious Virgin Mary with a glorious salutation, most fittingly consummated her blessedness by saying, *"Blessed art thou among women,"* that is, more blessed than all women. And by this, whatever of malediction was infused into our nature by Eve, was taken away by the blessing of Mary. Let Gabriel therefore say: "Blessed art thou among women"; blessed, I say, because of the fulness of grace to be venerated in thee; blessed, because of the greatness of the mercy to be bestowed by thee; blessed, because of the majesty of the Person who is to take flesh of thee; blessed, because of the weight of glory which is to be accumulated in thee.

First, consider how Mary is truly blessed because of the fulness of grace to be venerated in her, as Gabriel shows most aptly when he says: "Hail, full of grace, the Lord is with thee; blessed art thou among women." Blessed art thou, because thou art full of grace. Thou hast found grace with God, and therefore thou art blessed with the Lord. St. Bernard well says of this blessedness of Mary: "By thee we have access to thy Son, O blessed among women, finder of grace, Mother of life, Mother of salvation." Blessed art thou, O Mary, because of grace. Blessed, I say, because of the grace of the heart, of the lips, of the work. Blessed in heart, because of the grace of gifts; blessed in mouth, because of the grace of the lips; blessed in work, because of the grace of manners. Truly is Mary blessed because of the grace of the heart, for the grace of her gifts in her heart; for her heart was as the most delightful paradise of God, so that of this blessedness could be understood that word of Ecclesiasticus: "Grace is like a paradise in blessing." Here the commentary says: "Bearing fruit in the different species of virtues." Of these happy degrees and blessings of virtues the Apostle says: "Who hath blessed us in all spiritual blessings in the heavenly places in Christ." If, therefore, grace makes the mind of man delightful as the paradise of God in the blessings of virtues, how much more delightful must the soul of Mary be, that Paradise of God, in the blessings of the gifts of the Holy Spirit? Yea, verily, not only was the mind of Mary a Paradise of God, but also her bosom, containing within itself the tree of life, Jesus Christ. St. Bernard says: "Truly thou art the Paradise of God, who hast brought forth to the world the Tree of Life, of which he who shall eat shall live forever." Alas, how far from this blessedness of Mary is he whose mind is not a paradise of God in the blessings of grace, but a sink of the devils in the curse of malice! Of such is it said in the Psalm: "He loved cursing, and it shall come unto him: and he would not have blessing, and it was removed far from him" (Ps. CVIII, 18.)

Again, Mary is blessed, not only because of the gifts of her heart, but also because of the grace of her lips, according to that word of the Psalm: "Grace is poured abroad in thy lips, therefore hath God blessed thee forever." Oh, how great a grace was on the lips of Mary, in devout prayers, in useful conversations! Oh, how great a grace was always on the lips of Mary, for men, for angels, for the Lord! St. Bernard tells us how pleasing to God were the words of her lips, saying: "Him whom thou hast pleased by thy silence, thou shalt henceforth please much more by thy words, for He cries to thee from Heaven: 'O most beautiful of women, let me hear thy voice.'" Oh, how true, how sincere, were the lips of Mary, and therefore God truly hath blessed her forever. Oh, how far from the blessedness of Mary are they whose lips are so unlike hers, on whose lips grace is not poured, but malice; therefore, God hath not blessed, but cursed them forever.

Again, Mary is blessed not only because of the gifts of her heart and of her lips, but also because of the grace of her life and conversation. Of this blessedness can be understood what is said in Jeremias: "May the Lord bless thee, beauty of justice, holy mountain." The holy mountain is Mary, who is fitly called a mountain because of the loftiness of her life and manners. This is the mountain of which we read in Daniel: "A stone was cut out without hands" (Dan. II, 45.) This was when Christ was born of Mary without male co-operation. The beauty of this mountain is the beauty of justice. So great was the beauty of the life and manners of Mary that it could justly be said of her as in the Canticle: "Thou art all fair, O my beloved." She was beautiful indeed, in her life; beautiful in the discipline of her manners; and all beautiful. Without doubt all in her was beautiful. How all? Hear St. Jerome: "Whatever was in Mary, was all purity and simplicity, all grace and truth, all mercy and justice, which looked down from Heaven." Rightly did the Lord bless such beauty in Mary. Alas, how far are they from this blessing of Mary of whom it may be said, not what was said to Mary, "May the Lord bless thee, thou beauty of justice," but, "May the Lord curse thee, thou vileness of injustice!" Oh, what a malediction that will be when it will be said: "Depart from Me, ye cursed, into everlasting fire!" Behold, we have seen, O most dear Mary, that thou art truly blessed because of thy fulness of grace. Blessed, I say, because of the grace of conscience and of gifts; blessed, because of the grace of the tongue and of the lips; blessed, because of the grace of thy life and thy manners.

Secondly, consider how truly Mary is blessed because of the majesty of her heavenly Child, because of the blessed fruit of her womb. Rightly is that land blessed which produces so blessed a fruit. The Psalmist says: "Thou hast blessed, O Lord, thy land." That land is Mary, of whom it is said in the same Psalm: "Truth has sprung up from the earth." The Truth is Christ, who said: "I am the Way, and the Truth, and the Life." Blessed, therefore, is this earth, because of its blessed fruit; blessed is Mary, because of her blessed Son. Therefore St. Bernard says: "Not because thou art blessed, is the fruit of thy womb blessed; but because He hath prevented thee in the blessings of sweetness, therefore art thou blessed." Mary is blessed because of her Divine

Child. Blessed, I say, by the Lord, by the Angel, by man. Because of her Child she is indeed blessed by the Lord, who is Himself her blessing; blessed by the Angel, who announces her blessing; blessed by man, who prophesies her blessing. Truly is Mary blessed by the Lord because of her Child, who Himself is and gives her blessing. This is well signified in the second Book of Kings, where we read: "The Lord blessed Obededom because of the Ark." Obededom is interpreted "Servant of blood."

Well doth he signify Christ, who, having become our servant, serves us miserable sinners even unto blood. For our sake He became a slave, and shed His blood—the blood of His back by the scourge; the blood of His head by the thorns; the blood of His side by the lance; the blood of His hands and feet by the nails. The house of this servant is Mary, of whom it is said in the Psalm: "We shall be filled with the good things of His house." The ark placed in that house signifies Christ, for Christ is our servant and our life. In the ark was the golden urn and the manna. The holy ark is the sacred flesh; the golden urn is the precious soul of Christ; and the manna signifies His divinity. Because of this ark, because of Jesus Christ, the Son of Mary, the Lord blessed the house of Mary. O truly blessed house, from whence the life of all hath come forth! St. Augustine says: "Blessed art thou among women, who hast brought forth life to men and women."

Likewise, Mary is blessed because of her Child, not only by the Lord Himself being her blessing, but also by the Angel announcing her blessing. Gabriel says: "The Lord is with thee, blessed art thou among women." How "with thee"? St. Augustine explains: "With thee in heart, in the womb." Therefore, blessed art thou together with Him, because He is in thee and with thee. With thee, not only as the Creator is with His creature, but also as the Child is with her who is to bring Him forth. Because of thy Child, thou art blessed before thy delivery; because of thy Child, thou art blessed in bringing forth; because of thy Child, thou art blessed after bringing forth. Truly blessed art thou, who hast so brought forth thy Child that before His birth, and in His birth, and after His birth, thou hast remained a virgin; and therefore thou hast deserved to be called blessed, because thou hast brought forth not a mere man, not an angel, but the Lord of men and angels. Therefore St. Bede well says: "Truly art thou blessed among women, who without example in womankind rejoicest in the honour of a mother and the beauty of virginity, and as becomes a virgin-mother, thou hast given life to the Son of God."

Again, Mary is blessed because of her Child, not only by the Lord Himself being her blessing, not only by the Angel announcing her blessing, but by man prophesying her blessing. Elizabeth, when the infant in her womb exulted, cried out and said:

"Blessed art thou among women, and blessed is the fruit of thy womb." Therefore, thou art blessed indeed, because the fruit of thy womb is blessed; as a field is blessed because the fruit of it is blessed. Mary is that blessed field of which it is said: "Behold the smell of my son is as the smell of a plentiful field, which the Lord hath blessed" (Gen. XXVII, 27.) St. Jerome says: "Well is Mary called a full field, because she is said to be full of grace, from whose womb the Fruit of life came forth to all believers." O field truly blessed above all fields because of its fruit! O Mother truly blessed above all mothers because of thy Son! St. Augustine exclaims: "O Woman blessed above all women, who knew not man, yet encompassed a Man in her womb!" Behold we have seen, O most sweet Mary, that thou, because of the blessed Son of thy womb, art truly blessed with a divine blessing, an angelic blessing, and a human blessing! Alas, how far from this blessing of Mary are those who, because of the accursed fruit of their work, have incurred the divine malediction, the curse of angels and of men; for all eternity they will be cursed by God, cursed by angels, cursed by men.

Thirdly, think how truly Mary is blessed because of the multitude of her mercy. She is signified by Ruth, of whom it is said: "Blessed art thou by the Lord, because thy former mercy hath surpassed the latter." The former mercy of Mary was that which she showed while she still lived in this world; the latter mercy is that which she has now shown for centuries from Heaven. The latter blessing has surpassed the former, because she has exceeded it by an innumerable multitude of blessings. Who can reckon how inestimably Mary is blessed because of her mercy, when her mercy in itself is inestimable? And who can reckon how inestimable is the mercy of Mary, on account of which she herself is so inestimably blessed? St. Bernard says: "Blessed, therefore, is Mary for the manifold mercy which man received through her; blessed indeed, because by her, God was induced to be favourable to man; blessed is she also, because by her, man was made acceptable to God; blessed, moreover, is she, because by her, the devil was overcome." I say that Mary is blessed because by her, God was induced to be favourable to man, as is signified in the example of Abigail, of whom we read, that when David, being angry, wanted to kill the fool Nabal, Abigail, meeting him half-way, appeased him; who being appeased, said: "Blessed be thy speech, and blessed be thou, who hast kept me to-day from coming to blood, and revenging me with my own hand" (1 Kings XXV, 32 f.) The fool Nabal signifies the sinner; for every sinner is a fool. But, alas! as it is said in Ecclesiasticus: "The number of fools is infinite" (I, 15). Abigail signifies Mary, for the name is interpreted, "joy of the father." Oh, how great was the joy of the heavenly Father in Mary, and that of Mary in the heavenly Father, when she herself said: "My spirit hath rejoiced in God my Saviour." As Abigail typifies Our Lady, so David typifies Our Lord. For David was offended by the fool Nabal, when the Lord was offended by guilty man. David was appeased by the fool Nabal, when the Lord was appeased and reconciled to guilty man by Mary. Abigail appeased David by words and gifts; Mary appeased the Lord by her prayers and merits. Abigail turned away temporal vengeance, but Mary turned away that which was eternal; the former averted the sword of man, the latter, that of God. Therefore St. Bernard well says: "No one was so fitting, Lady, to turn away the sword of the Lord by their own hand, as thou, the most beloved of God, through whom we first received mercy from the hand of the Lord, our God." Likewise, Mary is blessed not only because by her God's wrath with man was appeased, but also because by her man was made acceptable to God, inasmuch as man was blessed because of her blessing. Therefore, is it well said in Isaias: "Israel will be a blessing in the midst of the earth, whom the Lord of hosts hath blessed, saying, 'Blessed be my people,'" etc. The middle of the earth which the Lord blessed can be said to be the Blessed Virgin, in whom was begun the blessing of our salvation, according to that word of the Psalmist: "But God our King hath wrought salvation in the middle of the earth." Of this middle of the earth, St. Bernard says: "With wonderful fitness is Mary called the middle of the earth; for towards her, as to the centre, as to the ark of God, as to the cause of things, as to the business of the world, look all those who dwell in Heaven and in hell, and those who have gone before us, and those who follow us. Those who are in Heaven, that they may be repaired; those who are in hell, that they may be delivered; those who went before, that prophets may be found trustworthy; those who follow, that they may be glorified." In this blessed middle of the earth, therefore, blessed is Israel, blessed is the people of God, since by the blessed Mother of God, it is acceptable to God. What wonder if by the blessed Mary every rational creature is blessed and acceptable to God, since by her is blessed every creature? Therefore St. Anselm exclaims: "O Virgin blessed, and more than blessed, by whose blessing every creature is blessed, not only the creature by the Creator, but the Creator by the creature."

Again, Mary is not only blessed because by her the Lord has been appeased towards man, but also because by her the devil has been rendered subject to man. She is, therefore, signified by Judith, of whom it is said: "The Lord hath blessed thee in his power, who by thee has reduced our enemies to nought." Our enemies are the demons, whom the Blessed Virgin reduced to nought when, in herself and in many others, she brought his wiles to nought, as St. Bernard says: "Thou formidable warrior"; and again: "The entire militia of evil spirits has been put to flight before thee." Let us, therefore, fly, and fly all together to the protection of the Mother of the Lord, in all the attacks and vexations of the devil. For she is terrible to the enemies of our souls, as an army in battle array. Alas, how manifold is our misery, for which we need the blessing and mercy of Mary. Let us, therefore, invoke this mercy and this blessing with St. Bernard, who speaks thus: "Let it be thine, O blessed Virgin, that grace which thou hast merited from God, to show to the world: pardon to the guilty, healing to the sick, strength to the faint-hearted, help and deliverance to pilgrims, by obtaining all these favours by thy prayers."

We have seen, O most sweet Mary, that thou art truly blessed because of thy manifold mercy. Blessed, I say, because by thee God is appeased towards man. Blessed art thou, because by thee man is made pleasing to God; blessed art thou, because by thee the devil is overcome by man. Alas, how far from this blessing of Mary is one who is not pleasing to God, one towards whom God's wrath is not appeased, one who is willingly subject to the devil. And therefore such a one is accursed of God.

Fourthly, consider how truly Mary is blessed because of the greatness of her glory, according to that word of Ezechiel: "Blessed is the glory of the

Lord from its place." The glory of the Lord is the glorious Mother of God, who is truly blessed because of the glory which she possesses from her twofold place. She is blessed from the place wherein she rests with her Son in Heaven; and she is blessed from the place wherein her Son rested within her. Both these places are most worthy, as St. Bernard proves, saying: "There was not in the world a more venerable place than the virginal bride-chamber into which Mary received the Son of God; nor in Heaven, than the regal throne to which the Son of Mary elevated Mary." Blessed is Mary, therefore, because of her glory; blessed indeed because of her most sublime, most copious, most enduring glory. Blessed, I say, because of her glory most sublime in dignity; blessed because of her glory most copious in immensity; blessed because of her glory most enduring in stability. I say that Mary is blessed because of her glory most excellent in dignity. Of this blessing can be understood that word of the Psalmist: "Thou shalt bless the crown of the year of thy kindness." Note that there is a year of equanimity, a year of severity, and a year of benignity. The first year is that of those still fighting in this world; the second is that of those weeping in hell; and the third is that of those rejoicing in Heaven. The first year has days and nights; the second has nights, but no days; the third has days, but no nights. I say that the first year has days and nights, that is, the good and the bad, who are still in this world. There are as many days and nights in this year as there are good and evil people in the world. The second year has nights only, that is, only sinners who are darker than night. For there are as many nights in this year as there are sinners in hell. The third year has only days, that is, the good, who are more resplendent than the day. There are as many days in this year as there are just souls in Heaven. In the first year, that of equanimity, the good and the evil are equally tolerated; in the second year, that of severity, the evil are most severely tortured; in the third year, that of kindness, the good are most benignantly crowned. The crown of this blessed year is the Virgin Mary. She is without doubt the crown of all the days of this year, for she is the crown of all the Saints in Heaven. A crown is put on the head; so Mary is, as it were, placed over the heads of all the Saints, as St. Jerome says: "She deserved to be placed above the choirs of the angels; and she went beyond what is of the nature of our lowliness." Without doubt the Son of Mary is the highest crown of the Saints; but Mary is a crown below a crown. It is manifest, therefore, how sublimely blessed is our crown, our Mother Mary. Let us all, therefore, follow her who is so sublimely blessed, blessed indeed, of whom St. Bernard says: "We have not here a lasting city, but we seek that to which Mary has blessedly attained."

Again, Mary is blessed, not only because of the

most excellent glory of her dignity, but because of the most abundant glory in immensity; its fulness is such that it is blessed by all men, and reaches to all, and, therefore, rightly is it blessed by men, according to what is said of it by figure in the Book of Judith: "They blessed her with one voice, saying: 'Thou art the glory of Jerusalem, thou art the joy of Israel, thou art the honour of our people.'" They all blessed her indeed. Note that they say *all*. For this there should be at least three. And there are three who bless Mary: God, the Angel, and man. God the Father indeed blessed Mary; the Son blessed His Mother; the Holy Ghost blessed her; all three Persons blessed her. The Angels also blessed Mary; the first hierarchy blessed her, the second also, and the third, all blessed her. Man also has blessed Mary; the married have blessed her; widows blessed her; virgins blessed her; all have blessed her. They have blessed her, saying: "Thou art the glory of the triumphant Jerusalem, the glory, I say, of all the Saints; thou art the joy of Israel, contemplating God; thou art the joy, I say, of all the angels; thou art the honour of our people who are still pilgrims, that is, thou art the honour of all the just who are in this world. Blessed, therefore, be thy most sweet Son, O Mary, who by thy abundant blessing bestows such good things on Heaven and on earth, so that the angels as well as men can rejoice with Anselm, and praise thee, saying: "These great gifts came through the blessed Fruit of the blessed womb of the blessed Mary."

Again, Mary is blessed not only because of her glory most sublime in dignity, not only because of her glory most abundant in immensity, but also because of her glory most enduring in stability. That is signified by the house, spoken of in the First Book of Paralipomenon: "Thou, O Lord, giving the blessing, it shall be blessed for ever." Truly forever, as it is said in the Psalm: "Therefore hath God blessed thee forever" (Ps. XLIV.) Thus, therefore, O sweet Virgin Mary, thou art truly blessed among women, and above women, yea also above men, nay, even above the angels. Blessed, I say, because of the fulness of grace which thou hast found; blessed, because of the majesty of the Person whom thou hast given birth to; blessed, because of the multitude of the mercies which thou hast shown; blessed, because of the greatness of the glory which thou hast received. Thee, therefore, O Blessed One, we invoke, we implore, we pray to thee with St. Bernard: "Grant, O blessed one, by the grace which thou hast found, by the prerogatives which thou hast merited, by the mercy which thou hast brought forth, that He who through thee deigned to become a partaker of our weakness and misery, may, by thy intercession, make us sharers of His heavenly glory. Amen."

CHAPTER XV

MARY IS BLESSED BY THE SEVEN VIRTUES AGAINST THE SEVEN CAPITAL VICES

Blessed art thou among women. Let us still speak of the blessing of our Blessed Virgin, let us still hear of it. Happy is the Blessed Mary; unhappy is every accursed soul to whom it shall be said: "Depart from me, ye cursed, into everlasting fire!" Cursed without doubt is every sinful soul, but blessed art thou, O virtuous Mary. The world incurred malediction by the seven capital vices; but Mary obtained blessing by the contrary virtues. Blessed, therefore, art thou among women, O Mary. Blessed by humility against pride, by charity against envy, by meekness against anger, by diligence against sloth, by temperance against gluttony, by chastity against lust.

First let us hear how Mary is blessed by humility against pride. For the proud are accursed, as it is written: "Thou hast rebuked the proud; cursed are they who decline from thy ways." Against this curse of pride Mary obtained the blessing of humility. Thus she may be signified by that valley of which it is said in Paralipomenon: "They called that place the valley of blessing" (2 Paralip. XX, 6.) If every humble soul is, as it were, a valley of God, according to that word of Isaias, "Every valley shall be filled," how much more was Mary a valley, who was so deep in humility! What wonder if she were the valley of valleys, who was the most humble of the humble? Oh, how greatly is this blessed valley exalted with blessings for her humility, so deep, so useful, so pleasing! St. Augustine says: "O truly blessed humility of Mary, who brought forth the Lord to men, gave life to mortals, renewed the heavens, purified the world, opened paradise, and delivered the souls of men from hell." The deeper a valley is, the more is it a receptacle for waters; so was Mary for graces. A valley receives irrigation by waters, sometimes from above, sometimes from below; from above, when the rains flow down from the mountains; from below, when there are springs of water in it. In like manner the humble Mary received waters, as it were, both from above and from below; she was, as it were, irrigated from a mountain and from a spring, when from the divine and from the human nature of her Son so great a blessing of graces was poured into her. This is that blessing of which we read in the Book of Judges, when Axa said to her father: "Give me a blessing." Her father gave her a place well watered from above and from below. Axa was a type of Mary, who received a well-watered blessing from the heavenly Father. For God the Father gave her a blessing from above in the divinity of Christ, and from below in His humanity; again from above in her mind, and from below in her womb; from above in her charity to God, from below in her love for her neighbour; again from above in contemplation, from below, in action. Or the heavenly Father gave her an ineffable blessing, from above in Heaven, from below on earth, that in Heaven she might possess the blessing of glory, and on earth that of grace; and thus be blessed both in Heaven and on earth, according to what St. Bernard intimates when he says: "Remember, O Mary, that Christ bore the malediction of the cross, who blessed thee, His Mother, in Heaven. But thou wert blessed also on earth by the Angel, and art rightly called blessed on earth by all generations."

Secondly, let us hear how Mary is blessed for charity against envy. The envious are accursed, as it is said of the envious Cain: "Cursed art thou upon earth, which has opened its mouth, and received the blood of thy brother from thy hand." Against the curse of envy, Mary has received the blessing of charity. She may well, therefore, be signified by Sara, of whom the Lord said: "I will bless her, and out of her I will give thee a son, whom I will bless" (Gen. XVII, 16.) Sara is interpreted as "coal." This is well suited to Mary, who, like a coal, was on fire with the ardour of charity. Therefore, the burning bush is a fit figure of Mary, by whom the blessing of grace is ministered to every faithful soul. It is said in Deuteronomy: "The blessing of him, who appeared in the bush, may it come upon the head of Joseph." Joseph is interpreted as "increase," and signifies every faithful soul enriched by divine grace. Blessed is the bush, and blessed is He who by His Incarnation appeared in the bush, by whom so great a blessing came upon the faithful. O truly blessed coal, producing so blessed a flame, blessed Mary bringing forth so blessed a Child. "From her," saith the Lord, "I will give thee a son, whom I will bless" (Gen. XVII, 16.) Think, therefore, what great charity Mary had towards God, when God is her Son according to the flesh. Think also what charity she had towards her neighbour, when the good neighbour is spiritually her son. And if we are her sons, we are the brethren of her Son. Well, therefore, doth St. Anselm say of this blessed Mother: "O blessed and exalted one, not for thyself alone, but also for us, what is it, how great is it, how lovable, what we see happening by thee for us, which, seeing, I rejoice, which, rejoicing, I dare not utter? For if thou, O Lady, art the Mother of God, are not thy other sons the brethren of God?"

Thirdly, hear how Mary is blessed for her meekness and gentleness against anger. For the angry are accursed, as it is written in Genesis: "Cursed be their fury, for it was stubborn: and their wrath, because it was cruel" (Gen. XLIX, 7.) Against this curse of wrath, Mary obtained the blessing of meekness. For truly her meekness was such that not only had she no anger of her own, but she even turned the anger of God to meekness. Therefore, she is well signified by Abigail, to whom David said: "Blessed be thy speech, and blessed be thou, who hast kept me to-day from coming to blood and revenging me with my own hand" (1 Kings XXV, 32.) It is the property of meekness to soothe with kind words the anger of those who are offended, according to that word of Proverbs: "A mild word turneth away anger" (Prov. XV, 1.) The meek Abigail signifies the meek Mary. Do you wish to know how meek Mary was? Listen to St. Bernard: "Turn over," he says, "diligently in your mind the whole of the Gospel story, and if you note in Mary anything of rebuke, anything hard, or even the slightest sign of indignation, you may perhaps suspect her in other things, and fear to approach her. But if you find that in all things she was rather full of grace and loving kindness, full of meekness and mercy, give thanks to Him who with such kind compassion has provided thee with such a mediatrix, in whom thou hast nothing to fear." David signifies Christ, who by Mary's meekness is soothed and placated, lest He should take vengeance on the sinner by eternal death. Let every soul in danger of eternal death never cease to sigh to Mary in her great meekness, for which she is rightly so blessed. I say, therefore: Let every soul about to die say with St. Anselm: "O thou blessed above women, who conquerest the angels by thy purity, surpassest the Saints by thy loving kindness, let my dying soul sigh at the sight of such great kindness; but let it blush at such resplendent whiteness."

Fourthly, hear how Mary is blessed by her diligence against sloth. For the slothful are accursed, because they do not do the work of God faithfully and earnestly. Jeremias says: "Cursed is he who doth the work of God negligently." Against the curse of torpor, Mary deserted the blessing of earnestness. For she may be signified by that Jahel, who killed Sisara with a nail. Therefore, in the Book of Judges it says: "Blessed is Jahel among women." Jahel is interpreted as "going up," which suits Mary, who did not, like the slothful, go down, but most earnestly always ascended from virtue to virtue, from a lower to a higher grade, according to that word of the Canticle: "Who is this who cometh up from the desert, like a rod of incense?" What has this blessed Jahel done? She killed Sisara with a nail. Sisara is interpreted as "the shutting out of joy," and well does this signify the devil, because he himself, being shut out from eternal joy, tries also to keep others out of it. Alas, yes, by means of the first mother of the human race he excluded all of us, and the curse of this exclusion was lifted by the Mother of our Saviour. Well, therefore, does the Venerable

Bede say: "Blessed art thou among women, by whose virginal bringing forth the curse of the first mother was excluded from those born of women." But what is signified by the nail wherewith the head of Sisara was pierced? What is this nail but severity of discipline? What is strictness of life to the lazy, but a sort of nail through the eyes? Strictness of discipline is, as it were, a nail painfully transfixing the devil, and sharply wounding him. The blessed Jahel, therefore, pierced the head of Sisara with that death-dealing nail, while the blessed Mary extinguished in herself the strength of Satan by strictness of discipline. Blessed, therefore, is Jahel among women, blessed is Mary among women. Among which women? Listen to Bede, who says: "Not only art thou blessed among women, but among women who are blessed thou art eminent by a greater blessing."

Fifthly, hear how blessed is Mary by her liberality against avarice. For the avaricious are accursed, as St. Peter says: "Having their heart exercised with covetousness, children of malediction" (2 Pet. II, 14.) Against this curse of avarice, Mary merited the blessing of generosity and profusion. For she was like a fountain ever flowing and ever giving, and therefore was truly blessed, according to that word: "Let thy vein be blessed" (Prov. V, 18.) In temporal things Mary, that vein, was more than generous, because she generously and liberally despised all things. Therefore, according to Haymon, the Blessed

Mother of God had the moon beneath her feet because she despised all temporal things. Oh, how great graces have flowed on to men by means of this vein! Therefore, O Church, thy vein be blessed, by whom so great good gifts have come to thee. Truly a noble vein, a vein full of the Holy Ghost, a vein the fountain of life; Mary is to us a vein of salvation. For by this vein Christ, the fountain of life, came to us, and by this vein we come to Jesus Christ, who is the fountain of life; truly, therefore, is it blessed. St. Bernard says: "By thee, O blessed finder of grace, we have access to God, Mother of life, Mother of salvation, that by thee He may receive us, who by thee was given to us."

Sixthly, hear how Mary is blessed by temperance against gluttony. For the gluttons are accursed, as it appears in the greediness of our first parents, for which both they and the whole human race incurred a curse. Against this curse of gluttony Mary obtained the blessing of abstinence and of every kind of temperance. Rightly indeed, in opposition to the curses of gluttony in the material paradise, did the blessings of temperance abound in the spiritual paradise, according to that word of Ecclesiasticus: "Grace is like paradise in blessings." So great an abundance of grace was in Mary that she, the gracious Virgin, might almost be called grace itself. This grace, that is, the most gracious Virgin Mary, was as a paradise in blessings. For as in the material paradise the gluttony of Eve merited the curses of punishments, so in the spiritual paradise the temperance of Mary merited the blessings of graces. Therefore Augustine says: "The curse of Eve was turned into the blessing of Mary." As the gluttony of Eve brought forth a curse not only in the body, but also in the soul, so Mary obtained for us a blessing not only in the body, but also in the soul; not a spiritual blessing alone, but likewise a corporeal one. The malediction of the greedy Eve was to bring forth in pain; the blessing of the temperate Mary was to bring forth without pain, as St. Bernard says: "Blessed art thou among women, thou who hast escaped that general curse, in which it is said: 'In sorrow thou shalt bring forth children,' and yet at the same time too that other, 'Cursed is the sterile in Israel'; and thou hast obtained a singular blessing, that thou shouldst neither remain sterile nor bring forth in sorrow."

Seventhly, let us hear how Mary is blessed by her chastity against lust. To the lustful it is said: "Cursed is he who shall sleep with the wife of his neighbour; and all the people shall say, Amen." Against this curse of incontinence, Mary merited the blessing of continence, as it may be signified in the Book of Judith, where we read: "They all blessed her with one voice, saying: Thou art the glory of Jerusalem, thou art the joy of Israel, thou art the honour of our people: for thou hast done manfully, and thy heart has been strengthened because thou hast loved chastity, and after thy husband hast not known any other: therefore also the hand of the Lord hath strengthened thee, and therefore thou shalt be blessed for ever" (Judith XV, 10 f.)

In this blessing of the chaste Judith, the blessing of Mary may not only be signified, but by this passage we may pass to a higher conclusion. If such was the blessing of a chaste widow, how much more will be that of a chaste virgin? And above all, of such a virgin as merited to bring forth God, and to do this in such a manner as not to lose her virginity. Well therefore doth Bede say: "She is incomparably blessed, who both received the glory of the divine seed, and kept the crown of virginity." Note, however, that in Scripture we find a blessed wife, a blessed widow, and a blessed virgin. The blessed wife was Sara, of whom it is said in Tobias: "A blessing was pronounced over the wife of Tobias." The blessed widow was Judith, as we have pointed out. Of a blessed widow it is also said in the Psalm: "Blessing I will bless his widow." And the blessed virgin was Mary, as the Angel testifies, saying: "Blessed art thou among women." She is blessed, therefore, because she was a wife; she is more blessed because she was a widow; she is blessed above all those who loved virginal chastity. She is blessed without doubt, who, like Sara and Susanna, was chaste in wedlock; she is more blessed, who, like

Judith and Anna, was a chaste widow; she is blessed above all, who with Mary shall have been chaste as a virgin. Therefore St. Augustine says: "We praise Susanna as a model of conjugal chastity; but we prefer before her the virtue of the widow Anna, and much more that of the Virgin Mary." This is truly meet and just. It is just that *she* should be blessed who had known no other man than her husband; it is more just that *she* should be blessed who neither during her husband's life-time nor after his death had known any man. It is meet and just that *she* should be blessed above all who neither knew her own, nor any other man, yet conceived a Man so supreme. Therefore St. Augustine exclaims: "O woman blessed above women, who knew no man, yet encompassed a man in her womb!"

Thus, therefore, was Mary deservedly blessed for her humility, for her charity, for her meekness, for her diligence, for her liberality, for her sobriety, for her chastity; she who was most excellent in humility, most rich in charity, most patient in meekness, most fervent in diligence, most temperate in sobriety, most continent in virginity. Thus, therefore, thou who art so manifoldly blessed, thou more than blessed Mary, let us pray that by thy blessing thou mayest free us wretched ones from every curse, and mayest make us worthy of the divine blessing, through Our Lord Jesus Christ. Amen.

CHAPTER XVI

WHO AND WHAT WAS THE FRUIT OF THE WOMB OF BLESSED MARY

Blessed is the fruit of thy womb. It has been shown above how Mary, because of the innocence of her life, is rightly saluted by the *Ave;* how because of the abundance of her grace, she is called full of grace; how because of the familiar presence of God with her it is said that the Lord is with her. We have now to show how, because of the most useful excellence of her Child, the Fruit of her womb is called blessed. Blessed, therefore, is the Fruit of thy womb, O Blessed Mother of the Son of God! This is that Fruit of which the Prophet saith: "The Lord will give benignity, and our earth will give its fruit." Commenting on this passage, Bede says: "The Lord gave benignity, because, by the entrance of His Only Begotten Son, He consecrated by the grace of the Holy Ghost the temple of the virginal womb. And our earth will give its fruit, because the same Virgin, who had her body from the earth, brought forth a Son, co-equal indeed in divinity with God the Father, but in the reality of His Flesh consubstantial with *her*." We have to consider, that this Fruit is a most well-born Fruit, a most delicious Fruit, a most virtuous and most abundant Fruit. A Fruit, I say, most sublime in being well-born, most desirable in delight, most useful in virtue, most universal in its abundance.

First, consider how the Fruit of the virginal womb is most well-born. It is well-born, because it is from a regal womb; it is more well-born because it is from a virginal womb; but it is without doubt most well-born because it is from the paternal womb, that is, from the womb of the Eternal Father. I say that this Fruit is well-born because it proceeds from a regal womb, that is, from the womb of King David, as the Lord had promised him, saying in the Psalm: "Of the fruit of thy womb I will place upon the throne." The Apostle bears witness to this in his letter to the Romans: "Who was made from the seed of David according to the flesh." Without doubt this Fruit is well-born and noble, not only because of King David, but because of all those noble kings, his progenitors, by whom, according to the genealogy described by Matthew, He came into this world, according to that word of Wisdom: "He came from a royal throne" (Wisd. XVIII, 15.) Again, this Fruit, although it is well-born because of the regal womb, is even more well-born because of the virginal womb, of which it is said: "Blessed is the fruit of thy womb," of that womb which, according to what is signified by the rod of Aaron, retained the flower of virginity together with the fruit of fecundity. Therefore, St. Bernard says: "Christ is born of a woman, but one to whom the fruit of fecundity came in such a manner that the flower of virginity did not fall." This nobility of the virginal fruit, as it is more wonderful, so it is also more excellent than the former, as far as the heavens are above the earth. O truly wonderful and unheard-of nobility! O truly noble birth from the Virgin! "The nobility of the Child was in the virginity which brought Him forth," says St. Augustine, "and the nobility of the parent was in the Divinity of the Child." Again, this Fruit is well-born because of the regal womb which bore it; more well-born because the womb was virginal; most well-born of all, because of its fatherhood. We can understand of this Fruit that word of Osee: "From me is thy fruit found to be" (Osee XIV, 9.) The original text has "thy," but the Septuagint has "hers." Let God the Father, therefore, say to Mary: let Him say to the faithful soul, let Him say to the Church: "From Me is thy fruit." Thine, O Mary, chosen to produce this fruit; thine, O soul, who art drawn to love this Fruit; thine, O Church, gathered together to partake of this Fruit. Thine, without doubt in the body by the nature He assumed; thine spiritually by grace; thine sacramentally by the Eucharist; thine eternally by glory. But it is of me that He is thine, because He was begotten from my womb, as it is written in the Psalm: "From the womb, before the day-star I have begotten thee." O truly wonderful and venerable nobility, that the fruit of the maternal womb is the Son of the Eternal Father, and the Wisdom of the paternal Heart, as St. Bernard says of this Fruit: "O Mary, thou wilt be the Mother of Him whose Father is God; the Son of the paternal love will be the crown of thy chastity; the Wisdom of the paternal heart will be the fruit of the virginal womb." The nobility of this most well-born fruit precedes in dignity the first and the second in an infinite degree, and exceeds by its sublimity every intellect, both human and angelic. Well, therefore, is it said of this fruit by Isaias: "There will be a bud of the Lord in magnificence and glory, and a sublime fruit of the earth"; in magnificence, because of the regal dignity; in glory, because of the virginal dignity; and it will be sublime, because of the eternal or paternal generosity.

Secondly, let us consider how the Fruit of the virginal womb is most delightful. It is delightful in smell, more delightful in appearance, but most delightful in savour. Its beauty is in faith, its odour in hope. We perceive its beauty by faith, its fragrance by hope, its savour by charity. I say that the Fruit of Mary is delightful by its sweet fragrance. Therefore, the Mother of this Fruit can well say with Ecclesiasticus: "I like a vine have borne a fruit of sweetness of odour." The fruit of the vine is the

Child of the Virgin. But what is truly wonderful, and wonderfully true, as says St. Augustine, speaking of this fruit: "The Creator of all things is born of a creature, a great fountain flows from a little rill, the root of all things springs from its stem, and the true vine is the fruit of its own branch." The fruit of the vine is wine; the smell of wine is delightful. So without doubt the fragrance of the examples of Christ, the fragrance of the consolations of Christ, the fragrance of promises of Christ, is most delightful to the soul that thirsts for Christ. And, therefore, as the smell of wine draws one who thirsts, so does the odour of Christ draw one who runs and says: "Draw me after thee," etc. That we miserable ones do not run, but creep, is a sign that we little relish the sweet odour of this Fruit. Oh, that we had Isaac's sense of smell, who perceived the odour of this divine fruit from such a distance; as St. Bernard says: "He perceived the fragrance of this sweet-smelling fruit, who said: Behold the smell of my son is as the smell of a full field, which the Lord hath blessed." Again, this Fruit is not only delightful to the sense of smell, but it is more delightful in beauty and fairness. Note on this point what is said in Leviticus: "Ye shall take on the first day the fruit of the most fair tree." The first day illumining the soul is faith. And certainly, if we ought to eat the Fruit of the most beautiful tree, that most fair tree is Mary; fair indeed in the leaves of the words of her mouth; fairer in the flowers of her heart; fairest of all in the most beautiful Fruit of her womb. Of which St. Bernard well says: "If that fruit of death was not only sweet to the palate, but also, according to Scripture, 'delightful to behold'; how much more should we seek the vivifying beauty of this life-giving Fruit, on which the angels long to look? Christ indeed is a beautiful Fruit, beautiful in form above the sons of men." But if we wish to appreciate more fully the beauty of this Fruit, let us have recourse to the beautiful tree itself, let us seek that most beautiful Mother herself, and let us speak to her that word of the Canticle: "What manner of one is thy beloved of the beloved, O thou most beautiful of women?" And behold she will at once answer: "My Beloved is white and ruddy, chosen from thousands." He, the brightness of eternal light, is indeed white in His divinity, but ruddy in His humanity, white in His life, ruddy in His Passion. Behold how beautiful is this Fruit! Well, therefore, doth St. Augustine say of Him: "Beautiful in Heaven, beautiful on earth, beautiful as the Word in the Father, beautiful in His Mother as the Word and as Flesh." And this most beautiful tree, Mary, has not only the most beautiful Fruit of the womb, but also the most beautiful Fruit of the mind. Of these fruits the Apostle, writing to the Galatians, says: "The fruit of the spirit is charity, joy, peace, patience, benignity, goodness, longanimity, mildness, faith, modesty, continence, and chastity." Again, this fruit is not only delightful in fragrance, and more delightful in beauty, but it is also most delicious in savour. This was felt by that holy soul who says: "I sat under the shadow of Him whom I desired, and His fruit was sweet to my palate." What wonder if this Fruit is so sweet, which is also so high? For St. Bernard says: "The higher a fruit is, the sweeter it is." Therefore, thou alone art most sweet, because thou alone art Most High. But how can that fruit be most high, whose tree is most short? But without doubt this tree, which is Mary, is at the same time most high and most short. She is most high in dignity, most lowly in humility; most high in the eyes of the Lord, most lowly in her own; although in this manner she is lowly, her fruit is nevertheless exceedingly sweet. Therefore is it said in Ecclesiasticus: "The bee is small among flying things, but her fruit hath the chiefest sweetness" (XI, 3.) If, therefore, the fruit of Mary is most delicious in fragrance, in appearance, and in savour, therefore is it truly blessed, as St. Bernard testifies, saying: "Blessed is the fruit of thy womb": blessed in smell, blessed in savour, blessed in beauty.

Thirdly, consider that the fruit of the virginal womb is most powerful. It has great power to save the lost, to multiply the number of those who are to be saved, and to preserve this great number. I say that this blessed fruit is powerful to save, or powerful unto salvation, and for this reason it is called the Fruit of salvation. Ecclesiasticus says: "The fear of the Lord is the crown of wisdom, filling with peace and the fruit of salvation." Why does he say, peace and fruit? The fruit of our salvation and our peace is He who maketh both one, Jesus Christ. And certainly, the fear of the Lord did fill this fruit, this peace, as Isaias says: "And He was filled with the spirit of the fear of the Lord." Well is He called the Fruit of salvation, without whom we have no salvation, according to that word: "There is no salvation in any other." And St. Anselm says: "There is no salvation except Him whom thou, O Virgin, hast brought forth." Thou, therefore, O Mary, art truly the tree of salvation, who hast borne for the world the Fruit of salvation, as St. Bernard says: "O truly celestial plant, more precious than all, more holy than all! O truly a tree of life, which alone was worthy to bear the fruit of salvation!" But, alas, there are many who make this life-giving fruit one of death; they turn this fruit, which is so sweet, so to speak, into an eternal wormwood for themselves, as it is said in Amos: "Ye have turned judgment into bitterness, and the fruit of justice into wormwood." Again, this fruit is exceedingly powerful, not only with a saving power, but with a multiplying power. We could explain it well perhaps by that word which is written, "By the fruit of their wheat, wine and oil they are multiplied," if we say that the wheat is the Body of Christ, the oil the soul of Christ, and the wine the Divinity of Christ. We can see in the fruit of the wheat the Sacrament of the Body of Christ, in the fruit of the wine the Blood of Christ in the Sacrament, and in the fruit of the oil the unction of the Holy Spirit. By this fruit sons are multiplied to the Church, and the Church is multiplied in sons. For all the sons of the womb of the Church are the inheritance and the fruit of the womb of Mary, as it is said in the Psalm: "Behold, the inheritance of the Lord is sons, the fruit of the womb." Of this St. Jerome says: "The Lord Himself, born of the Virgin, became the fruit of the womb, whose assumed humanity obtained this reward, that the nations called to be His sons should be His inheritance." Again, this blessed fruit is powerful not only in its salvific virtue, not only more powerful by its multiplying power, but also most powerful by its preserving virtue. Of this fruit we may understand that word of the Proverbs: "The fruit of the just is the tree of life." For, as the tree of life, which was in the middle of the earthly paradise, had power to preserve the life of nature, so without doubt the fruit of Mary's womb, which is the Tree and the Fruit of Life, in the midst of the Paradise of the Church, preserves the life of grace; in the midst of the Paradise of the heavenly life, preserves the life of glory. It preserves the life of grace from the corruption of guilt, and the life of glory from the corruption of every misery, that so we may receive in the fruit of Mary what we lost in the fruit of Adam and Eve, as Bede well says: "Blessed is the fruit of the womb of her by whom we have received the fruit of the seed of incorruption in the field of the eternal inheritance, which we had lost in Adam." Let, therefore, the fruit of Mary by spiritually giving salvation, by universally multiplying those who are to be saved, by eternally preserving those who are multiplied, be most powerful.

Fourthly, consider how the fruit of the virginal womb is most abundant. It is, in fact, so abundant that it can abundantly refresh the soul; it is so abundant that it can suffice for all; it is so abundant that it can never fail. In the first it is abundant; in the second it is more abundant; in the third it is most abundant of all. I say that this blessed Fruit is so abundant that it can refresh to satiety the rational soul, which the whole world and every creature cannot satisfy. Therefore it is written: "Of the fruit of thy works the earth shall be filled" (Ps. CIII, 13.) The fruit of the womb of Mary is the fruit of thy works, O Lord: indeed, of Thine, not of human beings, not of mortals, but of Thine. Thine, O Lord, is the work of the preparation of so much power; Thy work is the mission of Gabriel; the supervention of the Holy Ghost is Thy work; the union of the Word with Flesh is Thy work. Of such works of

Thine, O Lord, is this fruit, because from such works proceeded this fruit, as it were from flowers. Therefore aptly did these flowers appear in Nazareth, which is interpreted as "flower." For St. Bernard says: "In Nazareth is it announced that Christ will be born, because of the flower is hoped the coming of the fruit." The earth which is filled with this fruit is human nature, which, like the earth, is ever ready to germinate either useful or noxious plants, that is, thoughts and desires. This earth, I say, is filled with the fruit of Mary, as is written: "I shall be satisfied when thy glory shall appear." What wonder if those enjoying this fruit in glory are satisfied, when even those in misery here below are satisfied in believing in it! Therefore Cassiodorus cries out: "Oh, that wonderful Fruit, which has satisfied the human race in sweet belief!" Not to taste of it is to sin. See, therefore, how abundant this Fruit is, which can satisfy the soul, which the whole world cannot satisfy. Again, this Fruit, this blessed Fruit, is not only so abundant that it can fully refresh the insatiable soul, but it is also so abundant that it can well suffice for the whole number of those who are to be saved. Hence it is the fruit of that glorious tree of which it is said: "Its fruit was exceeding much; and in it was food for all" (Dan. IV, 9), certainly for all those who live in the Lord, those who rest and those who rise again, as it may be beautifully signified in Leviticus, where it says: "I will give you my blessing in the sixth year, and it will bring forth the fruit of three years" (Lev. XXV, 21.) The sixth year signifies the sixth age, the seventh the seventh age, and the eighth the eighth. This sixth year is the year of fulness, according to the Apostle: "But when the fulness of time was come, God sent His Son," etc. This year, therefore, brought forth the Fruit, the Son of God—a Fruit so abundant, that by it, in the sixth year of the living, in the seventh year of the dead, and in the eighth year of those rising again, we have all the fruit of our souls. He, therefore, is the Fruit sufficing to the universality of souls, because it is the Lord who suffices to all creatures. This indeed is the Fruit of the womb of Mary, as St. Augustine testifies, saying: "This Virgin was prevented and filled by a singular grace, that she might have Him for the fruit of her womb, whom from the beginning all things had as their Lord." Again, this blessed Fruit is not only abundant in this that it can fill to repletion all souls who are to be refreshed; it is not only more abundant in this that it can satisfy all the souls who need to be refreshed; but it is also most abundant in this that it can never fail in satisfying souls and angels, according to that word of Ezechiel, "Its fruit shall not fail" (Ezech. XLVII, 12.) O infinite abundance! O abundance which knows no defect! The abundance of this Fruit can never fail, for it is most abundantly blessed forever. St. Bernard says: "Blessed is the Fruit of thy womb, who is blessed forever." Thus this blessed Fruit is abundant, for it refreshes unto complete satisfaction; it is more abundant, because it suffices to the whole multitude of those who are to be fed upon it; it is most abundant because it never fails those who feed upon it, nor ever will for all eternity. You see now, O reader, O hearer, how exceedingly well-born, how exceedingly delicious, how exceedingly abundant is the blessed Fruit of the womb of Mary. You see, I say, how it is well-born because it is from a regal womb, more well-born because it is from a virginal womb, most well-born from its paternal origin. You see also how it is delightful in smell, more delightful in beauty, and most delightful of all in savour. You see how powerful it is to heal, more powerful in multiplying, most powerful of all in preserving. You see, moreover, how it is abundant to satisfy, more abundant in its universality, most abundant in its perpetuity. These twelve conditions or qualities of this Fruit may be signified by those twelve fruits of which it is said in the Apocalypse, that the angel showed John a tree of life bearing twelve fruits. And because this Fruit, the Fruit of life, the tree of life, is produced for the life of all men, therefore it is fitting and right that all men should praise the Maker of this Fruit in the words of the Psalm: "Let all peoples praise thee, O God, let all peoples praise thee; the earth hath given its fruit" (Ps. LXVI, 7.) O blessed Mother of this blessed Fruit, grant us that we may enjoy this fruit forever, by the same Fruit, Jesus Christ Our Lord, thy Son. Amen.

CHAPTER XVII

TO WHOM THE FRUIT OF THE WOMB OF THE BLESSED MARY BELONGS, AND TO WHOM IT IS DUE

Benedictus fructus ventris tui. After we have seen, in some small measure, of what kind and how great the Fruit of the womb of Mary is and is believed to be, let us now see to whom it belongs and to whom it is due. For this Fruit is not only the fruit of the womb, but of the mind. It is the fruit of the womb of Mary alone; but it is the fruit of the mind of any faithful soul; the fruit of the womb according to the flesh; the fruit of the mind by faith. Therefore St. Ambrose says: "If, according to the flesh, one only is the Mother of Christ; nevertheless, according to the mind, Christ is the fruit of all. For every soul conceives the Word of God, if only it is immaculate and immune from vices." Therefore, according to St. Ambrose, anyone who wishes to have this fruit of the mind, should be free from all vice. For Christ is the fruit of the virtuous, not of the vicious mind: not of the mind vicious by the seven deadly sins; but virtuous against the seven capital vices. Therefore, this fruit is the fruit of the humble against pride, the fruit of those possessing fraternal love in opposition to envy, the fruit of the meek as opposed to anger, the fruit of the diligent as against sloth, the fruit of the liberal as opposed to avarice, the fruit of the temperate as against gluttony, the fruit of the chaste against lust.

First, let us see how this blessed fruit is that of the humble against pride. On this we may understand what is said in the Book of Kings: "Whatsoever shall be left of the house of Juda, shall take root downward, and bear fruit upward" (4 Kings XIX, 30.) The Blessed Virgin Mary was of the house of Juda, and every faithful soul is of the house of Juda; the former in the body, the latter in spirit; the former by blood, the latter by faith. And, therefore, not only Mary, but every faithful soul wishing to bear fruit upward, should take root downward. The root sending its shoots downward is humility; which, after the manner of roots, always tends to the lowest. The higher the tree, the deeper should be its root, according to that word of Ecclesiasticus: "The greater thou art, the more humble thyself in all things, and thou shalt find grace before God." Also, the taller a tree is, the more danger there is of its being uprooted by the winds of elation, if the root is not firmly fixed in great and deep humility. Let us, therefore, ponder how deeply the root of this rod was established (in humility), which was to grow to so sublime a height that it deserved to bear a fruit higher than the angels, that fruit indeed of which St. Ambrose says: "This fruit is the flower of the rod, of whom Isaias says: 'There shall come forth a rod from the root of Jesse, and a flower shall ascend from its root.'" Whatever soul shall have struck deeply the roots of humility, shall deserve to bear fruit upward; upward, I say, in high understanding, in high affection; upward in contemplation, upward in love. Thus this blessed fruit is that of the humble. Therefore Mary, above all human beings, was most worthy, because of all she was the most deeply rooted in humility. Well, therefore, doth St. Bernard say of her: "O Virgin, rod sublime, to what a height dost thou raise thy holy summit! Even unto the throne of majesty, because thou strikest deep down the root of humility."

Secondly, let us see how this blessed fruit is that of those who love God and fly envy. Of this we can understand the word of the Psalmist: "Behold the inheritance of the Lord, the fruit of the womb." Commenting on this passage, St. Ambrose says: "The inheritance of the Lord is sons, which reward is the fruit of Him who came forth from the womb of Mary." Therefore, many sons are the reward of that only Son, who is the blessed fruit of the womb. But where or when did He merit that reward? Without doubt He merited it in being born, in lying in the manger; He merited it in bearing to be circumcised, in teaching; He merited it in doing the works of our salvation; He merited it by dying; He merited it, I say, in serving for us for thirty-three years. And because of this, He justly exacts this reward, saying: "If it seems good in your eyes, bring my reward" (Zach. XI, 12.) But without doubt it is not only sons who are the reward of the Fruit of the womb; but this Fruit of the most holy womb is Himself the reward of every son of adoption. Who are these sons? Listen and hear. It belongs to sons to love their father, and to the father to love his sons. Those, therefore, are sons of God and of the Church, who ever love God and their neighbour. Therefore, the Apostle says to the Ephesians: "Be ye imitators of God, as most dear children, and walk in love." And in St. Matthew it is said: "Love your enemies, do good to those that hate you, and pray for those that persecute and calumniate you, that you may be the children of your Father, who is in Heaven," etc. Such sons as these, therefore, that is to say, lovers of God and of men, are the reward of the Fruit of this blessed womb, and the reward of sons such as these is this blessed Fruit itself. Thus, therefore, is this Fruit that of those who love; and Mary above all men was most worthy of this Fruit, because she was the most affectionate in charity. Well, therefore, does St. Augustine say: "Who can doubt that all the bowels of Mary had passed into the love of charity, since within her rested for nine months that charity which is God?"

Thirdly, let us see how this fruit of Mary is that of those who are meek and patient and avoid anger. It is said in the Book of Job: "Submit thyself then to him, and be at peace, and thereby thou shalt have the best fruits" (Job. XXII, 21.) To submit and to be at peace belongs to the meek and to the patient; and those who are meek and patient have the best fruits by these very virtues. But the best fruit of the mind is charity, of which the Apostle says: "Now the fruits of the Spirit," etc. The fruits which are here enumerated are some, indeed, which are good, but there are some which are better; the first is best, namely, charity, by which all the others, as St. Augustine says, are good. The best Fruit of the womb is Christ: for whoever is sanctified in the womb, is the good fruit of the womb: therefore, good is the fruit of the womb of Elizabeth—John; better is the fruit of the womb of Anne—Mary; best is Jesus, the Fruit of the womb of Mary. Ponder, brother, who is this fruit, and from what earth it was produced, and thou shalt see that it is the best. St. Jerome says: "The fruit is a Virgin from a virgin, the Lord from the handmaid, God from man, the Son from the Mother, the fruit from the earth." O happy ones, who in the discipline of every sort of trial have a soul so patient, so just, so well prepared, that because of this they most justly reap the fruit of patience, that most peaceful fruit of which St. Paul says in the Epistle to the Hebrews: "Now all chastisement for the present indeed seemeth not to bring with it joy, but sorrow; but afterwards it will yield, to them that are exercised by it, the most peaceable fruit of justice" (Heb. XII, 11.) Having had their patience tested, they reap the best fruit, according to St. Luke: "They bring forth fruit in patience." As this blessed fruit is that of the patient and the meek, Mary above all men was most worthy of this fruit, because she was above all most meek, so that neither in looks, nor in word, nor in deed did she ever show the very slightest sign of impatience, but was most patient, as St. Ambrose says: "There was nothing fierce in the looks of Mary, nothing prolix in her words, nothing unbecoming in her deeds."

Fourthly, let us see how the fruit of Mary is that of those who labour and are diligent, and fly sloth. Of this it is said in the Book of Wisdom: "Glorious is the fruit of good works." This fruit, therefore, is to be sought by labour, as the bee seeks the fruit of honey; that fruit of which Ecclesiasticus says: "Small among flying things is the bee, and her fruit has the first sweetness." Consider, how the bee flies from garden to garden, from flower to flower, from tree to tree, in search of the fruit of honey; so do thou in meditations, in desires, and zealous imitation of virtues, exercise thyself about the examples of the just, and principally of the perfect. Fly, I say, from garden to garden, that is, from state to state; run from tree to tree, that is, from one just soul to another; from flower to flower, that is, from one virtue to another, from one good example to another. Above all, ruminate chiefly upon that flower in which you will find the whole fruit of the divine honey, upon that flower which is both flower and fruit, of which St. Ambrose says: "The Flower of Mary is Christ, who, like the fruit of a good tree, for our progress in virtue now bears fruit in us."

Note that this fruit is not of any labours whatsoever, but only of good works; it is not of those labours of which we read in the Book of Wisdom: "He that rejecteth wisdom and discipline, is unhappy: and their hope is vain, and their labours without fruit, and their works unprofitable" (Wisdom III, 11.) Thus is this blessed fruit that of those who exercise themselves in good and fly sloth. And therefore Mary above all human beings was most worthy of this fruit, because above all she was most diligent in good, as Bede well shows, when, in discoursing on the Magnificat, he puts these words into her mouth: "I offer the whole affection of my soul in the praises of thanksgiving; all my life, all that I feel, all that I discern in contemplating His magnitude, all this I employ in observing His precepts."

Fifthly, let us see how the fruit of Mary is of those who are liberal and fly avarice—principally of those generous souls who for the sake of this fruit renounce all temporal things, according to that word in the Canticle of Canticles: "Every man bringeth for the fruit thereof a thousand pieces of silver" (Cant. VIII, 11.) The commentator says, "by leaving all things." And again he says: "By 'a thousand' perfection, by 'silver' every worldly thing is meant." Whoever, therefore, has left all worldly things for Christ, as it were gives a thousand pieces of silver for this fruit. But he who is unwilling to give a thousand by leaving all things, let him at least give something for this fruit, by helping the poor, that he may be as the fruit-bearing olive by bearing the fruit of mercy. Because the highest fruit of mercy is the highest mercy, which is God; therefore Mary, who bore this fruit of mercy most abundantly, was most fittingly said to be like a fruit-bearing, a beautiful olive-tree in the fields. St. John Damascene well says: "Mary, planted in the house of the Lord and nourished by the Holy Ghost like a fruit-bearing olive-tree, became the dwelling-place of every virtue." Alas, how far from this fruit of mercy of the merciful, and of those detached from the love of earthly things, are the souls of the avaricious, of whom it is said: "Going their way they are choked with the cares and the riches and pleasures of this life, and yield no fruit" (Luke VIII, 14.) It is also said in Ecclesiastes: "He that loveth riches, shall reap no fruit from them" (Eccles. V, 9.) Thus this blessed fruit is of the liberal and of those who despise earthly things; and, therefore, Mary was above all most worthy of this fruit, because she was most generous in the contempt of temporal things, as St. Bernard says: "Whatever honour Mary had among her people, whatever she could have had of the riches of her father's house, she esteemed it all as dung, that she might gain Christ."

Sixthly, let us see how the fruit of Mary belongs to those who are temperate, and fly gluttony. And on this point we must note what is said by Solomon: "Of the fruit of his own mouth shall a man be filled with good things" (Prov. XIII, 2.)

The fruit of Mary can be said to be the fruit of the mouth, because it is acquired not only by the prayer of the lips and by teaching, but also by abstinence. With this fruit he is filled with spiritual things who for the sake of this fruit abstains from temporal goods. He shall be satisfied with the good things of this fruit who bears in his body hunger and thirst, but who hungers and thirsts spiritually with more eagerness for this fruit. Therefore St. Bernard says: "This is a good fruit, which is meat and drink to the souls who hunger and thirst after justice." It is well for those who thirst for this fruit in the world, because they shall be satisfied with it in Heaven, according to that word of the Saviour: "Blessed are ye who thirst now, for you shall be filled." Here the blessing is for those who abstain for the sake of this fruit, there it will be for those who eat of this fruit. Wherefore Isaias says: "Say to the just, that it is well; for he shall eat of the fruits of his doings" (Is. III, 10.) Thus this blessed fruit is of those who are temperate and fly gluttony, and therefore Mary above all human beings is most worthy of this fruit, for she was the most temperate and shunned gluttony. Well, therefore, does St. John Chrysostom say: "Mary was never a great eater nor given to wine; she was not light, nor frivolous, not a loud talker, nor a lover of evil words; these things are always the consequence of intemperance."

Seventhly, let us see how the fruit of the womb of Mary belongs to the chaste and continent who fly lust. Of this the Wise Man says: "Happy is the barren; and the undefiled, that hath not known bed in sin, she shall have fruit in the visitation of holy souls" (Wisd. III, 13.) I say, in the visitation by grace, but more so in the visitation by glory. And truly, the fruit of the most chaste womb, of the virginal womb, is rightly the special fruit of those who are chaste. When, therefore, by the blessed fruit of the Virgin all the faithful in general are blessed, rightly the chaste are specially blessed by Him, by whom also the blessed Queen of the chaste is blessed above all, as St. Bernard says: "Truly blessed is the Fruit of thy womb, in whom all nations are blessed: of whose fulness thou, too, hast received with the rest, and also differently from the rest." Woe to the lustful, who have no part in the virginal fruit: woe to the wretched, who have no branch which can bear a virginal fruit. Therefore is it said of the adulterous woman: "Her branches will not bear fruit" (Eccli. XXIII, 35.) Therefore does this blessed fruit belong to the chaste, who fly lust. And therefore Mary was above all worthy of this fruit, because she was most chaste, as St. Chrysostom well says: "O ineffable praise of Mary, Joseph trusted more to her chastity than to her womb, and more to grace than to nature; he rather believed it possible for a woman to conceive without a man, than that Mary could sin." O Mary most happy, who truly, as the most virtuous one, wast most worthy of the divine fruit, help us, that by our virtues we may be worthy to attain to this fruit, Our Lord Jesus Christ, thy Son. Amen.

CHAPTER XVIII

TO WHOM THE RESULTS OF THE FRUIT OF THE WOMB OF MARY ARE NECESSARY, AND OF ITS TWELVE ADVANTAGES

Blessed is the fruit of thy womb. We have seen of what nature and quality the blessed fruit of the womb of Mary was; we have also seen to whom it rightfully belongs; we must now see to whom and to what effects it is needful. For this fruit is a remedy against evil, and it is necessary for good. It is necessary in six of its effects as a remedy against evil; and it is necessary in six other effects for the attainment of good. For this blessed fruit has twelve very useful effects, or remarkable advantages, on account of which all men rightly praise its effects, according to what is written in the Psalm: "Let all peoples praise thee, O God, let all peoples praise thee: the earth has given her fruit" (Ps. LXVII.) The first effect of this fruit is the expiation of mortal sin; the second is the pacification of the supreme enmity; the third is the healing of the wound of original sin; the fourth is the satisfying of the hunger of the mind; the fifth is the avoidance of the anger of the Judge; the sixth is deliverance from the pains of hell; the seventh is the renunciation of temporal goods; the eighth is the enrichment of the rational soul; the ninth is the consummation of the spiritual life; the tenth is the multiplication of the universal Church; the eleventh is the reintegration of the empyreal ruin; the twelfth is the perpetuation of eternal glory.

First, therefore, the blessed fruit of Mary is necessary for the expiation of mortal sin. Of this we can understand what is said in Isaias: "This is the whole fruit, that sin may be taken away" (Is. XXVII, 9.) By the whole fruit we may understand Him of whom St. Bernard says: "On the cross hangs all the fruit of life, because the tree of life itself is in the midst of Paradise." All the fruit, therefore, is the whole fruit, the whole of Him. This Fruit was given, born, and suffered that the sin of man might be taken away. For, as the Angel said: "He hath saved His people from their sins." He also is the one of whom John spoke: "Behold the Lamb of God, who taketh away the sins of the world!" This Lamb truly takes away the sins of the world, both mortal and venial. He who by this fruit is purged from mortal sins, may also be cleansed from venial sins, according to the word: "Every one who beareth fruit, He will purge, that he may bring forth more fruit."

Secondly, the blessed fruit of Mary is necessary for the removal of the mortal enmity which existed between God and man, between angels and men. Isaias says: "I created the fruit of the lips, peace, peace to him that is far off, and to him that is near" (Is. LVII, 19.) The fruit of the womb of Mary may well be called the fruit of the lips of Mary, because while from her lips distilled the honey-flowing words, "Behold the handmaid of the Lord, be it done unto me according to thy word," she immediately conceived her most sweet Fruit. O truly honey-flowing lips, as it is said in the Canticle: "Thy lips are as the dropping honeycomb." It was God the Father who created this fruit, which is Our Lord Jesus Christ, or who made [in Him] peace; peace, I say, to him who is afar, by guilt, that he may become near by grace, and peace to him who is near by grace, lest he should be made far by guilt. For He, as the Apostle says, is "our peace, who maketh both one." This fruit also was made peace between man, who is far distant in this world, and the angel, who in Heaven is near; for Christ made peace with both on the gibbet of the Cross, according to the word of the Apostle: "Making peace by the blood of his Cross, both those things which are in Heaven and those which are on earth." Therefore, this fruit is peace from man to man, peace from man to the angel, and peace between God and man. What wonder if by this fruit man has peace with God, when He Himself, the peace-giving Fruit, is both God and man? Bede gives testimony to this, saying: "Our earth will give its fruit, because the Virgin Mary, who had her body from the earth, brought forth a Son in divinity indeed, co-equal with the Father, but consubstantial with herself in the reality of His flesh."

Thirdly, this blessed fruit of Mary is necessary for the healing of the wound of original sin; for man, falling among thieves, was wounded with a grievous wound, nay, many grievous wounds, while by original sin he became so blind to the truth, so infirm in good, so prone to evil. But these wounds are healed by this fruit. In this life indeed they are only partially healed by grace; but in the future life they will be entirely healed in glory. Therefore, well is it said in the Apocalypse: "The Angel showed John the tree of life, bearing its fruits every month, and the leaves of the tree were for the healing of nations." The tree of life is Mary, the Mother of Life; or the tree of life is the tree of the Cross; or else the tree is Jesus Christ, the Author of Life, who is also the Fruit of Life. Those healing leaves are edifying words and deeds. If even the leaves are healing, how much more healing and life-giving is the fruit? Therefore, that we may be healed by this fruit, let us approach its tree; let us draw near, I say, to Mary. Let us pray with St. Anselm: "Hear me, O Lady! Heal the soul of thy servant who is a sinner, by virtue of the blessed Fruit of thy womb, who sitteth at the right hand of his Almighty Father."

Fourthly, the blessed fruit of Mary is necessary for the relief of hunger, or the famine of the soul, lest for want of due nourishment the animals of God should perish. Therefore it is well said by the Prophet Joel: "Fear not, animals of the region, for the beautiful places of the desert have blossomed, and the tree has brought forth its fruit." It is a desert or a wilderness because it germinates without culture, and brings forth food for animals. This desert may signify Mary, who without marital culture brought forth a Son, who is the food of all the faithful. Therefore it can be said of her: "That earth is uncultivated, it has become as a garden of pleasure" (Ezech. XXXVI, 35.) The beautiful blooms of this uncultured earth are the flowers of heavenly desires, the grasses of good works, the fair flowers of virtues and gifts, the lovely leaves of useful words, and the truly beautiful fruit of Mary's womb, which is the food of all the just. Mary is this beautiful desert. Mary is also this fruitful tree, of which it is said: "And the tree brought forth its fruit" (Joel II, 22.) Oh, truly wonderful fruit, by which both the hunger and the thirst of souls is relieved, as St. Bernard says: "Good Fruit, which is food and drink to hungering and thirsting souls." Do not fear, therefore, animals of God; fear not, ye faithful of Christ, that you will perish from want of food, because you have full pasture in the desert, full fruit on the tree, full food in the manger." For St. Bernard says: "The Child lies in the manger, that all the faithful—as it were, the beasts of burden —may find refreshment for their flesh." St. Augustine says: "O resplendent manger, in which has lain the food of animals, but also the food of angels!"

Fifthly, the blessed fruit of Mary is necessary for the avoidance of the anger of the Judge, which every unjust man has to fear, in the same way as every just man has by right that by which he may escape the anger of the Judge. Therefore it is said in the Psalm: "If indeed there is fruit to the just, God indeed judging them on earth," etc. "Them," that is, the unjust, for God will judge the unjust upon earth, while at the judgment the just will be in the air, but the unjust will remain upon the earth, because they preferred to cleave to earthly things instead of God, so that they could truly say: "My soul hath cleaved to the pavement." There the Lord will be indeed a sweet fruit to the just, but to the unjust and wicked he will be a severe judge. Woe, therefore, to them who turn so sweet a fruit into a most bitter judgment for themselves, as it is said in Amos: "You have turned judgment into bitterness, and the fruit of justice into wormwood" (Amos VI, 13.) The fruit of justice is the fruit of the just. Just is the fruit of Mary, of whom the

Psalmist truly says: "The just has borne fruit. The earth is the virgin, because truth has sprung forth from the earth."

Sixthly, the blessed fruit of Mary is necessary for the avoidance of the pains of hell, or eternal death, on which we can say that which we find in the fourth of Kings: "I will take you away to . . . a fruitful land, and plentiful in wine, a land of bread and vineyards, a land of olives, and oil and honey, and you shall live, and not die" (4 Kings XVIII, 32.) All those who will be converted to her with their whole heart shall be taken away into the land of Mary, or the land of the Church. This land is exceedingly fertile, bearing fruit of bread, wine, oil, and honey, that is, Our Lord Jesus Christ. For He is to us the fruit of bread which strengthens, and puts to flight defect or failure; He is to us the fruit of the vine, for all perfection; He is to us the fruit of oil, illuminating the intellect; and He is moreover to us the fruit of honey, instilling sweetness into our affections. By this fruit ye shall truly live, dearly beloved, and ye shall not die. Blessed is the earth of this fruit; blessed above all be this fruit itself, by whom we are delivered from so many evils, as St. Anselm well says: "What praise shall I give that is worthy of the Mother of my Lord and God, by whose fecundity I, a captive, have been redeemed, by whose Child I am delivered from eternal death, by whose offspring I, a lost one, am restored, and led back from exile to my fatherland?" Blessed among women, all these things Christ, the blessed fruit of her womb, has given me in the regeneration of Baptism. Woe, therefore, to all those who are estranged from this fruit, for it is written: "Every tree, that bringeth not forth good fruit, shall be cut down and cast into the fire."

Seventhly, the blessed fruit of Mary is necessary for the renunciation or contempt of earthly goods. Therefore, it is said in the Canticle: "A man shall give for this fruit a thousand silver pieces," namely, leave all things. For, as the Gloss says, a thousand means perfection, and silver means all worldly substance. Therefore, anyone who perfectly renounces all earthly riches for Christ's sake, gives as it were a thousand silver pieces for this fruit, and rightly does he despise for the sake of this fruit all temporal things whoever diligently marks how exceedingly precious is this fruit, saying that word of the Proverbs: "My fruit is better than gold and precious stones, and my jewels than chosen gold" (Prov. XVIII, 20.) He is truly a man who has such virility as this; and this man ought manfully, for the sake of this fruit, to contemn not only possessions and riches, but also honours and dignities, saying: "Can I leave my sweetness, and my delicious fruits, and go to be promoted among the other trees?" (Judges IX, 11.) Most sweet are the fruits of Christ, and charity. The trees of the wood, says the Gloss, are barren men, prepared for the eternal fire.

Therefore, for the sake of these most sweet fruits he manfully contemns most dangerous honours which promote him above the trees of the wood; he manfully contemns all things for the sake of this blessed fruit, which is blessed above all, God forever.

Eighthly, the blessed fruit of Mary is necessary for the enrichment of the rational soul. It is said in Proverbs: "Each one shall be filled with the fruits of his mouth" (Prov. XVIII, 20.) We confess that the Lord Jesus is truly not only the fruit of the womb, but also the fruit of the lips, because we obtain Him by the preaching of the mouth or lips, by the praise of the lips, and by the prayer of the lips. With the external mouth we receive Him sacramentally, with the inward mouth we receive Him spiritually. Therefore St. Jerome says: "The Flower of Mary became fruit, that we might eat of it." With this fruit of the lips each one shall be filled with the goods of spiritual riches, the goods, I say, of virtues and graces. Of such goods the Apostle says: "May the God of hope fill you with all joy and peace in believing, that you may abound in hope and in the power of the Holy Ghost." O truly blessed fulness of this fruit, with which was filled not only the field of the Virgin which produced it, but also the soul of every faithful Christian who contains it, as is manifest by what St. Jerome says: "Truly is she called a full field, for the Virgin Mary is said to be full, from whose womb the Fruit of life came forth to believers, and all of us of His fulness have received grace for grace."

Ninthly, the blessed fruit of Mary is necessary for the perfection of the spiritual life. Therefore it is well said in the Psalm of the perfect man: "And he shall be like a tree planted by the running waters," etc. What should we understand by the running waters but the streams of grace, by which man gives or produces his fruit, the Lord Jesus Christ. Three conditions of a perfect life are signified which accompany the man who has this fruit. It belongs to the perfect not to waste their time, therefore it is well said: "It will give its fruit in its time." It is also a sign of perfection nor to overflow in useless words, which we understand to be signified in the words, "and his leaf shall not fall off." It is also a characteristic of perfection not to omit those things which are profitable to the soul; hence we find, "and all that he shall do shall prosper." Truly anyone who shall bear this fruit by charity, shall find all things prosperous, for all things will work together unto good for him, as it is written: "We know that for those who love God, all things work together unto good." Blessed is the man who shall have borne this fruit so perfectly that he shall not pass his time uselessly, that he shall utter no idle word, that he shall let no opportunity of virtue pass, and so he shall be like the tree bearing fruit spiritually, as Mary did corporeally, of whom St. Bernard says: "O truly the

The Fruit of the Womb of Mary

tree of life, which alone was worthy to bear the fruit of salvation!"

Tenthly, the blessed fruit of Mary is necessary for the multiplication of the universal Church. Therefore is it said: "With the fruit of her hands she hath planted a vineyard" (Prov. XXXI, 16.) The Lord Jesus, as He is well said to be the fruit of the womb, because He was conceived in the womb, and as He is well said to be the fruit of the lips, because He is received in the mouth—so also is well said to be the fruit of the hands, because He is acquired by the labour of the hands in good works, and is ministered to the faithful by the hands of the priest. Therefore, this fruit is most fully the fruit of Mary: it is truly the fruit of her womb, because He was born in a most singular way from her womb. He is also the fruit of her mouth, because by her mouth He was most sweetly communicated. He is also the fruit of her hands, because by her hands He was most devoutly handled. Of this fruit of her hands, Mary, or the primitive Church, planted a vineyard, that is, the universal Church, which is diffused throughout the world. Oh, how the branches of this vine, that is, the faithful members of the Church, have been multiplied by this fruit, while the rulers of the Church have caused this fruit to be spiritually born in the hearts of the faithful! Hence it is well said in the Psalm: "They yielded fruit of birth, and He blessed them, and they were multiplied exceedingly" (Ps. CVI,

37-38.) And because the Church in all ages has been multiplied by this fruit, therefore, the Virgin producing this fruit is rightly called blessed by all generations. As she herself well says: "Behold from henceforth all generations shall call me blessed." St. Bernard explains these words as follows: "Behold I see what is to come to pass in me, what fruit shall come forth from me, how great and how many good things will come to pass, by means of me, not to me alone, but to all generations."

Eleventhly, the blessed fruit of Mary is necessary for the restoration of the empyreal ruin, the ruin, I say, brought about in the high Heaven. On this we may note what the Lord, wishing to plant of the marrow of a high cedar, said: "On the high mountains of Israel I will plant it, and it shall shoot forth into branches, and shall bear fruit" (Ezech. XVII, 23.) The high mountain is that sublime mansion, that sublime society of angels, which is well called the high mountain of Israel, because Israel is interpreted "the vision of God." And behold the angels always see God, as we find in the Gospel of St. Matthew: "Their angels always see the face of My Father, who is in heaven." On this high mountain, in this sublime society of angels, God planted that which He had chosen from the mass of perdition; He planted, I say, the marrow of a cedar, the marrow of the human race, that is, all the elect, of whom some, in reality, some in hope, are already planted on the angelic mountain. O fruit, truly to be loved above all things, on whose account every elect soul is planted on so sublime a height! We must joyfully bear this fruit, Our Lord Jesus Christ, for whose sake we are already planted in hope among the angels. Let us always give thanks to this fruit by whose grace we fill up the number of the angels. Therefore Mary, the Mother of this fruit, may well glory, and utter those words which St. Bernard, speaking as it were by her lips, says: "The number of the generations of the angels is by my Child filled up, restored, and the race of men, cursed in Adam, by the blessed fruit of my womb is regenerated unto eternal blessedness."

Twelfthly, the blessed fruit of Mary is necessary for the perpetuation of eternal glory, which would not be eternal, unless it was preserved by this fruit. Therefore, is it said in Proverbs: "The fruit of the just is a tree of life." Excellently is this fruit said to be a tree of life, because as the tree of life was to preserve the natural life in the terrestrial Paradise, so Christ is to preserve eternal life in the heavenly Paradise. St. Anselm notes all the good things which we obtain through the blessed fruit of Mary, and says: "All these good things came from the blessed fruit of the blessed womb of the Blessed Mary."

Thus you have heard how the blessed fruit of Mary is necessary, first, to expiate mortal sin; secondly, to placate the supreme enmity between God and man; thirdly, to heal the wound of original sin; fourthly, to relieve spiritual obstinacy; fifthly, to appease the anger of the Judge; sixthly, to escape the pains of hell; seventhly, to obtain the grace to despise earthly things; eighthly, to enrich the rational soul; ninthly, to consummate the spiritual life; tenthly, to multiply the universal Church; eleventhly, to repair the empyreal ruin; twelfthly, to preserve eternal glory. And behold, these twelve effects or advantages of this fruit may be signified by the twelve fruits of the tree of life, all of which are in the fruit of Mary's womb. Of which twelve fruits we read in the Apocalypse, that the Angel showed John the tree of life, bearing twelve fruits.

Help us, therefore, O blessed among women, that by the fruit of thy womb we may obtain the blessing of these twelve fruits. Help us, O fruitful Virgin, that by thy fruit we may be made fruitful in these fruits; that by these fruits we may merit to enjoy thy fruit forever! Help us, O sweetest one, that Jesus may grant us to enjoy His sweetness, He, the most liberal communicator of the blessed fruit of thy womb, who with the Father and the Holy Ghost liveth and reigneth world without end. Amen.

THE PSALTER OF THE BLESSED VIRGIN MARY

200[1]

---

[1] Blank page in the original

TRANSLATOR'S PREFACE

The following work, entitled *Psalterium Beatae Mariae Virginis,* St. Bonaventure composed on the plan of the Psalter of David. There are in it one hundred and fifty psalms, the initial verses of each corresponding to the psalms of David, but the verses following are adapted to the Blessed Virgin in a most beautiful manner. This Psalter also contains eight canticles, in the manner of the canticles of Isaias, Ezechias, Anna, the two of Moses, Habacuc, the three children in the fiery furnace, and Zacharias; besides the hymn, "We praise thee, O Mother of God," after the manner of the Te Deum of SS. Ambrose and Augustine; and finally, a Marian *"Quicumque vult"* in the style of the Creed of St. Athanasius.

The author explains his aim in his preface, which follows.

AUTHOR'S PREFACE

"Take hold on her, and she shall exalt thee: thou shalt be glorified by her, when thou shalt embrace her. She shall give to thy head increase of graces, and protect thee with a noble crown." (Prov. IV, 8-9.)

Glory be to God on high, and thanksgiving, and the voice of praise, who at one time by the mysteries of prophecy, at another by oracles from Heaven, again by the reading of the Gospel, and now by the mouth of preachers, in many ways and by divers channels, most sincerely urges and invites us to honour the Virgin Mary, the Queen of Heaven and of the Angels; that by her holy merits, most worthy of all acceptance, we, being delivered from the depths of hell, may be inscribed by her in the ranks of the angels. Wherefore, although Solomon spoke the aforesaid words of Wisdom, nevertheless the Holy Spirit, by a mystical application, intends them to be understood of the most excellent Virgin Mary.

By means of these words, dearly beloved, He is drawing you to His love, and by various promises is attracting and softening your hearts, that you may enjoy His divine embraces. His meaning is that you will obtain four wonderful gifts, if this glorious Virgin is joined to you by a spiritual bond, and is embraced by you in the arms of fervent desire, with great reverence and devotion. First, she will bring you exaltation; and she shall exalt thee; secondly, glorification; and thou shalt be glorified by her; thirdly, the abundance of graces; she shall give to thy head increase of graces; fourthly, the unfading crown of prepetual glory, and protect thee with a noble crown. Therefore I beseech thee, dearly beloved and most desired, do not repel so noble and so beautiful a virgin; do not make little of so admirable and revered a queen as the Virgin Mary: lest, if she should see herself despised by you, you will be, I will not say, deprived of such great favours, but, which God forbid, you will incur perpetual evils. Expand the bosom of your mind to serve her, prepare your heart to praise and glorify her, loose your tongue, and with swift service hasten to please her. For there is no doubt that from her nearness to you you will become more devout, from contact with her you will grow more pure, from her embrace you will abound more in grace and be more resplendent in purity. That I may give you an occasion of obtaining such great gifts, I send you the Psalter of this most Holy Virgin, put together and composed indeed by my feeble intelligence, but with her grace and help; by means of it you will praise with divers hymns, now her virginity and chastity, now her fecundity and sanctity, now her clemency and bounty. You will be able to salute her as full of all grace, or as filled with all knowledge, or as illumined by all understanding and wisdom. There you will bless the Fruit of her glorious womb, the members of His holy body, and the prerogatives of His soul, bestowing all sanctity. There you will invoke the aid of all the choirs of angels to praise her, and of all the multitudes of holy men, the isles of the nations, the heavens, the beauty of all luminaries and of the whole world. There you will beseech her to destroy the power of your spiritual enemies, to obtain for you pardon of all your sins, that she may render the great Judge propitious to you, that she may illumine your deathbed by her gracious presence, and obtain for you joy without end. Therefore, O dearly beloved souls, graciously receive this little gift which I offer you, and strive to draw fruit therefrom; by means of it frequently praise the Mother of God; and thus perchance she will turn to you her gracious countenance, receiving you to her love, refreshing your soul in the present, and placing upon your head a crown of precious stones in the world to come.

THE PSALTER OF THE BLESSED VIRGIN MARY

PSALM 1

Blessed is the man, O Virgin Mary, who loves thy name; thy grace will comfort his soul.

He will be refreshed as by fountains of water; thou wilt produce in him the fruit of justice.

Blessed art thou among women; by the faith of thy holy heart.

By the beauty of thy body thou surpassest all women; by the excellence of thy sanctity thou surpassest all angels and archangels.

Thy mercy and thy grace are preached everywhere; God has blessed the works of thy hands.

Glory be to the Father, etc.

PSALM 2

Why have our enemies raged and our adversaries devised vain things?

May thy right hand protect us, O Mother of God: as a line of battle terrible in aspect, confounding and destroying them.

Come ye to her, all who labour and are in trouble: and she will give refreshment to your souls.

Draw nigh to her in your temptations: and the serenity of her countenance will bring you peace and confidence.

Bless her with your whole heart: for the earth is full of her mercy.

Glory be to the Father, etc.

PSALM 3

O Lady, why are they multiplied who afflict me? By thy might thou shalt follow them and scatter them.

Loose the bands of our impiety: take away the burden of our sins. Have mercy on me, O Lady, and heal my sickness: take away the grief and anguish of my heart.

Deliver me not into the hands of my enemies: and in the day of my death strengthen thou my soul.

Lead me into the harbour of salvation: and give up for me my spirit to my Maker and Creator.

Glory be to the Father, etc.

PSALM 4

When I called upon thee, thou didst hear me, O Lady: and from thy throne on high thou hast deigned to be mindful of me.

From the roaring of the wild beasts prepared to devour me: and from the hands of them that sought me, thy grace will deliver me.

For thy mercy is kind and thy heart loving: towards all who invoke thy holy name.

Blessed art thou, O Lady, forever: and thy majesty for evermore.

Glorify her, all ye nations in your strength: and all ye peoples of the earth, extol her magnificence.

Glory be to the Father, etc.

PSALM 5

Incline thine ear, O Lady, to hear my prayers: and turn not away from me the beauty of thy face.

Turn our mourning into rejoicing: and our tribulation into joy. May our enemies fall down at our feet: by thy power may their heads be crushed.

Let every tongue praise thee: and let all flesh bless thy holy name.

For thy spirit is sweet above honey: and thy inheritance above the honey and the honeycomb.

Glory be to the Father, etc.

PSALM 6

Lady, let me not be corrected in the wrath of God: nor be judged by Him in His anger.

For the honour of thy name, O Lady: may the Fruit of thy glorious womb be propitious to us.

From the gate of hell and from the depths of the abyss: by thy holy prayers deliver us.

May the eternal gates be opened unto us: that we may declare forever thy wondrous works.

For it is not the dead, nor those in hell, who will praise thee, O Lady: but those who by thy grace will obtain eternal life.

Glory be to the Father, etc.

PSALM 7

O my Lady, in thee have I hoped: from my enemies deliver me.

Shut thou the mouth of the lion and his teeth: restrain the lips of those that persecute me.

For thy name's sake delay not to accomplish thy mercy in us.

May the brightness of thy countenance shine upon us: that the Most High may keep remembrance of us.

If the enemy should persecute my soul, O Lady, may I be strengthened by thy help: lest his sword should strike me.

Glory be to the Father, etc.

PSALM 8

O Lady, Our Lord has become our brother and our Saviour.

Like the flame in the burning bush, and the dew in the fleece: the Word of God descends into thee forever.

The Holy Spirit hath made thee fruitful: the power of the Most High hath overshadowed thee.

Blessed be thy most pure conception: blessed be thy virginal bringing forth.

Blessed be the purity of thy body: blessed be the sweetness of the mercy of thy heart.

Glory be to the Father, etc.

PSALM 9

I will praise thee, O Lady, with my whole heart: and I will declare among the nations thy praise and glory.

For to thee is due glory, and thanksgiving, and the voice of praise.

May sinners find grace with God by thee, the finder of grace and salvation.

May the humble penitents hope for pardon: heal thou the bruises of their hearts.

In the beauty of peace and wealth rest: thou shalt feed us after the toil of our pilgrimage.

Glory be to the Father, etc.

PSALM 10

I trust in our Lady; because of the sweetness of the mercy of her name.

Her eyes look upon the poor: and her hands are stretched out to the orphan and the widow.

Seek after her from your youth: she will glorify you before the face of the peoples.

Her mercy will deliver us from the multitude of our sins: and will bestow on us fruitfulness of merits.

Stretch out to us thy arm, O glorious Virgin: and do not turn away from us thy glorious face.

Glory be to the Father, etc.

PSALM 11

Save me, O Mother of fair love: fount of clemency and sweetness of piety.

Thou alone makest the circuit of the earth: that thou mayst help those that call upon thee.

Beautiful are thy ways: and thy paths are peaceful.

In thee shine forth the beauty of chastity, the light of justice, and the splendour of truth.

Thou art clothed with the sunrays as with a vesture: resplendent with a shining twelve-starred crown.

Glory be to the Father, etc.

PSALM 12

How long, O Lady, wilt thou forget me and not deliver me in the day of tribulation?

How long will my enemy be exalted above me? By the might of thy strength do thou crush him.

Open the eyes of thy mercy: lest our enemy prevail against us.

We magnify thee, the finder of grace, by whom the ages of the world are restored.

Thou art exalted above the choirs of angels: pray for us before the throne of God.

Glory be to the Father, etc.

PSALM 13

Our foolish enemy hath said in his heart: I will follow after and take him, and my hand shall slay him.

Arise, O Lady, and prevent him, and supplant him: destroy all his machinations.

Thy beauty astonishes the sun and the moon; the angelic powers serve and obey thee.

By thy gentle touch the sick are healed: by thy rose-sweet fragrance the dead revive.

Virgin Mother of God, He whom the whole world cannot contain was enclosed within thee, being made Man.

Glory be to the Father, etc.

PSALM 14

O Lady, who shall dwell in the tabernacle of God? or who shall rest with the leaders of the people?

The poor in spirit, and the pure of heart, the meek, the peaceful, and the mourners.

Be mindful, O Lady, that thou speak for us good things: and that thou mayest turn away the indignation of thy Son from us.

O sinners, let us embrace the footprints of Mary, and cast ourselves at her blessed feet.

Let us hold her fast, nor let her go: until we deserve to be blessed by her.

Glory be to the Father, etc.

PSALM 15

Preserve me, O Lady, for I have hoped in thee: do thou bestow on me the dew of thy grace.

Thy virginal womb has begotten the Son of the Most High.

Blessed be thy breasts, by which thou hast nourished the Saviour with deific milk.

Let us give praise to the glorious Virgin: whosoever ye be that have found grace and mercy through her.

Give glory to her name: and praise forever her conception and her birth.

Glory be to the Father, etc.

PSALM 16

Hear, O Lady, my justice and my love: remove from me my tribulations.

I will give praise to thee in the voice of rejoicing: when thou shalt magnify thy mercy in me.

Imitate her, ye holy virgins of God: as Agnes, Barbara, Dorothy, and Catherine have done.

Give honour to her by the voice of your lips: thus have Agatha, Lucy, Margaret, and Cecilia received her grace.

She will give you as your Spouse the Son of the Father: and a crown incomparably radiant with the lilies of Paradise.

Glory be to the Father, etc.

PSALM 17

I will love thee, O Lady of heaven and earth: and I will call upon thy name in the nations.

Give praise to her, ye who are troubled in heart: and she will strengthen you against your enemies.

Give to us, O Lady, the grace of thy breasts: from the dropping milk of thy sweetness refresh the inmost souls of thy children.

Honour her, O all ye religious: for she is your helper and your special advocate.

Be thou our refreshment, glorious Mother of Christ: for thou art the admirable foundation of the religious life.

Glory be to the Father, etc.

PSALM 18

The heavens declare thy glory: and the fragrance of thine unguents is spread abroad among the nations.

Sigh ye unto her, ye lost sinners: and she will lead you to the harbour of pardon.

In hymns and canticles knock at her heart: and she will rain down upon you the grace of her sweetness.

Glorify her, ye just, before the throne of God: for by the fruit of her womb you have worked justice.

Praise ye her, ye heaven of heavens: and the whole earth will glorify her name.

Glory be to the Father, etc.

PSALM 19

Thou shalt hear us, O Lady, in the day of tribulation: and by our prayers turn to us thy merciful countenance.

Cast us not off in the time of our death: but help the soul, when it shall have left the body.

Send an angel to meet it: by whom it may be defended from the enemy.

Show unto it the most serene Judge of ages: who for thy grace will bestow pardon.

Let it feel thy refreshment in its torments: and grant to it a place among the elect of God.

Glory be to the Father, etc.

PSALM 20

O Lady, in thy strength our heart shall rejoice: and in the sweetness of thy name our soul shall be consoled.

From thy throne send us wisdom: by which we shall be sweetly enlightened in all truth.

Give us grace to abstain from carnal desires: that the light of thy grace may arise in our hearts.

How sweet are thy words, O Lady, to them that love thee: how sweet is the shower of thy graces.

I will sing unto thy glory and honour: and in thy name I will glory forever.

Glory be to the Father, etc.

PSALM 21

O God, my God: let Him look at thy merits in me, ever Virgin Mary.

O my Lady, I have cried to thee by day and by night: and thou hast done mercy with thy servant.

Because I have hoped in thy mercy: thou hast taken away from me everlasting reproach.

Mine enemies have mocked me on every side: but thou under the shadow of thy hand hast bestowed good refreshment on me.

Let all the families of the peoples adore thee: and let all the orders of the angels glorify thee.

Glory be to the Father, etc.

PSALM 22

The Lord rules me, O Virgin Mother of God: because thou hast turned on me thy gracious countenance.

Blessed are thy most resplendent eyes: which thou deignest to turn on sinners.

Blessed is the light and the splendour of thy countenance: blessed is the grace of thy face.

Blessed be the mercy of thy hands: blessed be the stream of thy virginal milk.

Let the prophets and apostles of God bless thee: let martyrs, confessors, and virgins sing praise to thee.

Glory be to the Father, etc.

PSALM 23

The earth is the Lord's and the fulness thereof: but thou, O most holy Mother, reignest with Him forever.

Thou art clothed with glory and beauty: every precious stone is thy covering and thy clothing.

The brightness of the sun is upon thy head: the beauty of the moon is beneath thy feet.

Shining orbs adorn thy throne: the morning stars glorify thee forever.

Be mindful of us, O Lady, in thy good pleasure: and make us worthy to glorify thy name.

Glory be to the Father, etc.

PSALM 24

To thee, O Lady, have I lifted up my soul: in the judgment of God, by the help of thy prayers, I shall not be ashamed.

Let not my adversaries make game of me: for those who trust in thee are strengthened.

Let not the snares of death prevail against me: and the camps of the malignant not hinder my steps.

Crush their violence in thy might: and with mildness meet my soul.

Be my guide unto my fatherland: and deign to join me to thy angelic hosts.

Glory be to the Father, etc.

PSALM 25

Judge me, O Lady, for I have departed from my innocence: but because I have hoped in thee I shall not become weak.

Enkindle my heart with the fire of thy love: and with the girdle of chastity bind my reins.

For thy mercy and thy clemency are before my eyes: and I was delighted in the voice of thy praise.

O Lady, I have loved the beauty of thy face: and I have revered thy sacred majesty.

Praise ye her name, for she is holy: let her wonders be declared forever.

Glory be to the Father, etc.

PSALM 26

O Lady, may thy light be the splendour of my countenance: and let the serenity of thy grace shine upon my mind.

Raise up my head: and I will sing a psalm to thy name.

Turn not away thy face from me: for from my youth up I have greatly desired thy beauty and thy grace.

I have loved thee and sought after thee, O Queen of Heaven: withdraw not thy mercy and thy grace from thy servant.

I will give praise to thee in the nations: and I will honour the throne of thy glory.

Glory be to the Father, etc.

PSALM 27

To thee, O Lady, will I cry, and thou shalt hear me: in the voice of thy praise thou wilt make me glad.

Have mercy on me in the day of my trouble: and in the light of thy truth deliver me.

Blessed be thou, O Lady: to the uttermost ends of the earth.

The sanctuary which thy hands have established: is the holy temple of thy body.

Thy conscience is pure and undefiled: a place of propitiation and the holy dwelling of God.

Glory be to the Father, etc.

PSALM 28

Bring to Our Lady, O ye sons of God: bring to Our Lady praise and reverence.

Give strength to thy saints, O holy Mother: and thy blessing to those who praise and glorify thee.

Hear the groans of those who sigh to thee: and despise not the prayers of those who invoke thy name.

Let thy hand be ready to help me: and thy ear inclined to my prayer.

Let the heavens and the earth bless thee: the sea and the world.

Glory be to the Father, etc.

PSALM 29

I will exalt thee, O Lady, for thou hast taken me up: thou wilt deliver me from the wicked enemy.

Turn to me and quicken me, from the gates of death lead me back: and from the rivers of tribulation which have surrounded me.

For the sake of thy empire and the magnificence of thy right hand: break and scatter all my enemies.

And I will offer thee a sacrifice of praise: and I will most devoutly exalt thy glory.

Rejoice, ye Heavens, and be glad, O Earth: because Mary will console her servants and will have mercy on her poor.

Glory be to the Father, etc.

PSALM 30

In thee, O Lady, have I hoped, let me never be confounded: receive me in thy grace.

Thou art my strength and my refuge: my consolation and my protection.

To thee, O Lady, have I cried, when my heart was in anguish: and thou hast heard me from the heights of the eternal hills.

Thou shalt draw me out of the snares which they hid for me: for thou art my helper.

Into thy hands, O Lady, I commend my spirit: my whole life and my last day.

Glory be to the Father, etc.

PSALM 31

Blessed are they whose hearts love thee, O Virgin Mary: their sins will be mercifully washed away by thee.

Holy, chaste, and flowering are thy breasts: which blossomed into the flower of eternal greenness.

The beauty of thy grace will never see corruption: and the grace of thy countenance will never fade.

Blessed art thou, O sublime Rod of Jesse: for thou hast raised thyself unto Him who sits in the highest.

O Virgin Queen, thou thyself art the way by which salvation from on high hath visited us.

Glory be to the Father, etc.

PSALM 32

Rejoice, ye just, in the Virgin Mary: and in uprightness of heart praise ye her together.

Draw near unto her with reverence and devotion: and let your heart be delighted in her salutation.

Give unto her the sacrifice of praise: and be ye inebriated from the breasts of her sweetness.

For she sheds upon you the rays of her loving kindness: and she will enlighten you with the splendours of her mercy.

Her fruit is most sweet: it grows ever sweeter in the mouth and the heart of the wise.

Glory be to the Father, etc.

PSALM 33

I will bless Our Lady at all times: and her praise shall never fail in my mouth.

Magnify her with me: all ye who are nourished with the milk and honey of her refreshment.

In dangers and doubts invoke her: and in necessities you will find sweet help and refreshment.

Take example from her conversation: and be zealous to imitate her charity and humility.

Because thou wast most humble, O Lady: thou hast induced the Uncreated Word to take flesh from thee.

Glory be to the Father, etc.

PSALM 34

Judge, O Lady, them that harm me: arise against them and avenge my cause.

My soul will rejoice in thee: and I will devoutly exult in thy benefits.

The heavens and the earth are full of thy grace and sweetness: from every side thy kindness surrounds us.

For wherever we may walk: the fruit of thy virginal womb meets us.

Let us run, therefore, dearly beloved, and salute the noble Virgin overflowing with sweetness: that we may rest in the bosom of her sweetness.

Glory be to the Father, etc.

PSALM 35

The unjust man said that he would sin in secret: by thee let him depart from his impious purpose, O Mother of God.

Incline towards us the countenance of God: impel Him to have mercy.

O Lady, in heaven is thy mercy: and thy grace is spread abroad in the earth.

Power and strength are in thy arm: vigour and fortitude in thy right hand.

Blessed be thy empire over the heavens: blessed be thy magnificence upon the earth.

Glory be to the Father, etc.

PSALM 36

Be not angry with the wicked, O Lady: sweeten their fury by thy grace.

O ye religious and cloistered souls, hope in her: confide in her, ye priests and seculars.

Take delight in her praises: and she will grant the petitions of your heart.

Better is a little with her grace: than treasures of silver and precious stones.

Glory be to thee forever, O Queen of Heaven: and never forget us at any time.

Glory be to the Father, etc.

PSALM 37

O Lady, let not the Lord rebuke me in His anger: obtain for us pardon for our sins.

Let all our desire be in thy sight: our hope and our confidence.

My heart is troubled within me: light departs from my interior.

Enlighten with thy brightness my blindness: sweeten with thy sweetness my contrite heart.

Forsake us not, O Lady, Mother of God: let thy grace and thy power be at my right hand.

Glory be to the Father, etc.

PSALM 38

I said: I will keep my ways, O Lady: when by thee the grace of Christ was given to me.

By thy sweetness my soul was melted: my bowels are inflamed by thy love.

Hear my prayer, O Lady, and my supplication: and let mine enemies pine away.

Have mercy on me from Heaven and from the height of thy throne: and permit me not to be troubled in the valley of misery.

Keep my foot, lest it should be injured: and may thy grace be with my end.

Glory be to the Father, etc.

PSALM 39

Expecting, I have expected thy grace: and thou hast done with me according to the multitude of the mercies of thy name.

Thou hast heard my prayers: and thou hast led me out of the den of misery, and from the pit of the enemy.

Manifold and wonderful are thy gifts, O Lady: incomparable are the gifts of thy graces.

Let all those exult and rejoice in thee who love thee: let them who have hated thy name, fall into hell.

Blessed be thou forever, O Lady: forever, world without end.

Glory be to the Father, etc.

PSALM 40

Blessed Mary understandeth concerning the needy and the poor: who remains faithful in her praises.

Lady of the angels, Queen of the world: purify my heart with the fire of love and of thy charity.

Thou art the mother of the illumination of my heart: thou art the nurse who refreshes my mind.

My mouth longs to praise thee: my mind devoutly aspires to venerate thee with ardent affection.

My soul longs to pray to thee: because the whole of my being commends itself to thy guidance and teaching.

Glory be to the Father, etc.

PSALM 41

As the hart longs for the water-brooks, so doth my soul pine for thy love.

For thou art the mother of my life: and the sublime repairer of my flesh.

For thou art the feeder of the Saviour of my soul: the beginning and the end of all my salvation.

Hear me, O Lady, let my stains be cleansed: enlighten me, O Lady, that my darkness may be illuminated.

Let my tepidity be enkindled by thy love: let my torpor be expelled by thy grace.

Glory be to the Father, etc.

PSALM 42

Judge me, O Lady, and discern my cause from the perverse nation: from the malignant serpent and the pestiferous dragon deliver me.

Let thy holy fecundity scatter him: let thy blessed virginity bruise his head.

Let thy holy prayers strengthen us against him: let thy merits put to nought his strength.

Send the persecutor of my soul into the abyss: let the infernal pit swallow him alive.

But I and my soul will bless thy name in the land of my captivity: and I will glorify thee forever and ever.

Glory be to the Father, etc.

PSALM 43

O Lady, we have heard with our ears: and our fathers have told it unto us.

For thy merits are ineffable: and thy wonders exceedingly stupendous.

O Lady, innumerable are thy virtues: and inestimable are thy mercies.

Exult, O my soul, and rejoice in her: for many good things are prepared for those who praise her.

Blessed be thou, O Queen of the Heavens and the angels: and let those who praise thy magnificence be blessed by God.

Glory be to the Father, etc.

PSALM 44

My heart hath uttered a good word, Lady: it is sweetened with honey-flowing dew.

By thy sanctity let my sins be purged: by thy integrity may incorruption be bestowed upon me.

By thy virginity may my soul be loved by Christ: and joined to him by the bond of love.

By thy fecundity I, a captive, am redeemed: by thy virginal bringing forth I am delivered from eternal death.

By thy most worthy Son I, a lost one, am restored: and from the exile of misery I am led back to the homeland of beatitude.

Glory be to the Father, etc.

PSALM 45

O Lady, thou art our refuge in all our needs: and a most powerful force bruising and crushing our enemy.

The world is full of thy benefits: they surpass the heavens and penetrate the depths.

By the fulness of thy grace those who were in the abyss rejoice to find themselves liberated.

By the power of thy virginal fecundity, those who were above this world: rejoice to find themselves freed.

By the glorious Son of thy most holy virginity: men are made companions and fellow-citizens of the angels.

Glory be to the Father, etc.

PSALM 46

All ye nations, clap your hands: sing in jubilee to the glorious Virgin.

For she is the gate of life, the door of salvation, and the way of our reconciliation.

The hope of the penitent: the comfort of those that weep: the blessed peace of hearts, and their salvation.

Have mercy on me, O Lady, have mercy on me: for thou art the light and the hope of all who trust in thee.

By thy salutary fecundity let it please thee: that pardon of my sins may be granted unto me.

Glory be to the Father, etc.

PSALM 47

Great art thou, O Lady, and exceedingly to be praised: in the city of the God of Heaven: in the entire Church of His elect.

Thou hast ascended, hymned by the angelic choirs: buoyed by the archangels, crowned with lilies and roses.

Meet her, ye Powers and Principalities: go to welcome her, ye Virtues and Dominations.

Cherubim, and Thrones, and Seraphim, exalt her: and place her at the right hand of the Spouse, her most loving Son.

Oh, with how joyful a soul, with how serene an aspect hast thou received her, O God of angels and men: and given her the principality over every place of thy domination.

Glory be to the Father, etc.

PSALM 48

Hear ye these things, all ye nations: give ear, all ye who desire to enter the kingdom of God.

Honour the Virgin Mary: and ye will find life and perpetual salvation.

Keep thy poor servants, O Lady: join them with a happy union to Christ.

By the fruit of thy womb, refresh and sustain the hunger of thy little ones.

For after thy bringing forth thou hast remained incorrupt: and after thy Son, inviolate.

Glory be to the Father, etc.

PSALM 49

The God of gods hath spoken to Mary: by Gabriel, his messenger, saying:

Hail, full of grace, the Lord is with thee: by thee the salvation of the world is repaired.

The Son of the Most High hath greatly desired thy beauty and thy comeliness.

Adorn thy bridal chamber, O Daughter of Sion: prepare to meet thy God.

Thou shalt conceive by the Holy Ghost: who will make thy delivery virginal and joyful.

Glory be to the Father, etc.

PSALM 50

Have mercy on me, O Lady: for thou art called the Mother of Mercy.

And according to thy mercy: cleanse me from all my iniquities.

Pour forth thy grace upon me: and withdraw not from me thine accustomed clemency.

For I will confess my sins to thee: and I will accuse myself of all my crimes before thee.

Reconcile me to the Fruit of thy womb: and make peace for me with Him who has created me.

Glory be to the Father, etc.

PSALM 51

Why dost thou glory in malice: O malignant serpent and infernal dragon?

Submit thy head to the Woman: by whose power thou art plunged into hell.

Crush him, O Lady, with the foot of thy power: arise and scatter his malice.

Extinguish his might: and reduce his strength to ashes,

That living, we may exult in thy name: and with joyful soul we may give praise to thee.

Glory be to the Father, etc.

PSALM 52

The foolish enemy hath said in his soul: I will cast men out from the tabernacle of the sons of God.

I will go forth, and I will be a lying spirit in the mouth of the serpent: and by the woman I will cast out the man, her husband.

O wretched one, as the heavens are exalted above the earth: so are the thoughts of God above thy thoughts.

Be not lifted up because of the woman's fall: for it is a woman who shall crush thy head.

Thou hast prepared a pit for her: and in her snare thou shalt be caught.

Glory be to the Father, etc.

PSALM 53

O Lady, save me in thy name: and deliver me from my injustices.

That the craft of the enemy may not hurt me: hide me under the shadow of thy wings.

O my Lady, help me! bestow thy grace upon my soul!

Willingly I will offer thee a sacrifice of praise: and I will give praise to thy name, for it is good.

For thou shalt deliver me from all tribulation: and my eye shall despise mine enemies.

Glory be to the Father, etc.

PSALM 54

Hear my prayer, O Lady: and do not despise my supplications.

I am become sad in my thoughts: because the judgments of God have terrified me.

The darkness of death has overtaken me: and the fear of hell has invaded me.

But in solitude I will expect thy consolation: and in my chamber I will wait for thy mercy.

Glorify thy arm and thy right hand: that our enemies may be prostrated by us.

Glory be to the Father, etc.

PSALM 55

Have mercy on me, O Lady, for my enemies have trodden upon me every day: all their thoughts are turned to evil against me.

Stir up fury, and be mindful of war: and pour out thy anger upon them.

Renew wonders and change marvellous things: let us feel the help of thine arm.

Glorify thy name upon us: that we may know that thy mercy is forever.

Distil upon us the drops of thy sweetness: for thou art the cupbearer of the sweetness of grace.

Glory be to the Father, etc.

PSALM 56

Have mercy on me, O Lady, have mercy on me: for my heart is prepared to seek out thy will.

And I will rest in the shelter of thine arms: for sweet to me is thy refreshment.

Thy hands have distilled the first myrrh: and thy fingers the unguents of graces.

And a fragment of pomegranate is thy throat: and thy breath is sweet as an amalgam of choice smelling herbs.

For thou art the mother of fair love and the anchor of hope: the harbour of safety, indulgence or pardon, and the gate of salvation.

Glory be to the Father, etc.

PSALM 57

If indeed you will truly speak justice: honour the Queen of justice and mercy.

For this belongs to the praise and the glory of the Saviour: whatever of honour is bestowed upon the Mother.

The roses of martyrs surround thee, O Queen: and the lilies of virgins encompass thy throne.

Praise ye her, all together, ye morning stars: the seas and the rivers and the foundations of the world.

Glory be to the Father, etc.

PSALM 58

Deliver me from mine enemies, O Lady of the world: arise to meet me, O Queen of piety.

The purest gold is thy ornament: the sardine stone and the topaz are thy diadem.

The jasper and the amethyst are in thy right hand: the beryl and the chrysolite in thy left.

The hyacinths are on thy breast: shining carbuncles are the jewels of thy bracelets.

Myrrh, frank-incense, and balsam are on thy hands: the sapphire and the emerald on thy fingers.

Glory be to the Father, etc.

PSALM 59

O God, thou hast cast us off because of our sins: thou hast had mercy on us by the Virgin Mary.

Intercede for us, O saving Mother of God: who hast brought forth salvation for men and angels.

For thou infusest joy into the sad: and joy and sweetness into the mourners.

Rejoice us by the sweet sounds of thy speech: and pour thy balm of roses forth into our hearts.

Thunder, ye heavens, from above, and give praise to her: glorify her, ye earth, with all the dwellers therein.

Glory be to the Father, etc.

PSALM 60

Hear my prayer, O Lady: upon a firm rock establish my mind.

Be thou to me a tower of strength: protect me from the face of the cruel destroyer.

Be thou to him terrible as an army in battle array: and may he fall living into the depths of hell.

For thou art shining and terrible: a cloud full of dew, and the rising dawn.

Thou art beautiful and bright as the full moon: thy sacred aspect is as when the sun shines in its strength.

Glory be to the Father, etc.

PSALM 61

O Lady, shall not my soul be subject to thee: who hast brought forth the Saviour of all?

Be mindful of us, O saviour of the lost: hear thou the weeping of our hearts.

Pour forth graces from thy treasury: and with thine unguents soothe our grief.

Give us joy and peace: that thou mayest confound the enemies of the good.

Wash away all our sins: heal all our infirmities.

Glory be to the Father, etc.

PSALM 62

O God, my God: I will glorify thee by Thy Mother.

For she hath conceived thee in virginity: and without travail she hath brought Thee forth.

Blessed be thou, O Lady: stand for us before the throne of God.

Beauty and brightness are in thy sight.

Keep my soul, O Lady: that it may never fall into sin.

Glory be to the Father, etc.

PSALM 63

Hear my prayer, O Lady, when I beseech thee: from the fear of the cruel one deliver my soul.

Obtain for us peace and salvation: in the last day.

Blessed be thou above all women: and blessed be the fruit of thy womb.

Enlighten, O Lady, mine eyes: and illumine my blindness.

Give me firm confidence in thee: in my life and in mine end.

Glory be to the Father, etc.

PSALM 64

A hymn becometh thee, O Lady, in Sion: praise and jubilation in Jerusalem.

The Lord hath given thee the blessing of all nations: praise and glory in the sight of all peoples.

The Lord hath blessed thee in His mercy: and hath set thy throne above all the orders of angels.

He hath placed grace and beauty in thy lips: and with a mantle of glory he hath clothed thy body.

He hath set a resplendent crown upon thy head: and hath adorned thee with the jewels of virtues.

Glory be to the Father, etc.

PSALM 65

Shout with joy to Our Lady, all the earth: sing ye a psalm to her name: give honour to her majesty.

Blessed be thy heart, O Lady: with which thou hast ardently and sincerely loved the Son of God.

Look upon my poverty, O glorious Virgin: delay not to remove my misery and my difficulties.

Take away my tribulations: sweeten my weariness.

Let all flesh bless thee: let every tongue glorify thee.

Glory be to the Father, etc.

PSALM 66

May God have mercy on us and bless us: by her who brought Him forth.

Have mercy on us, O Lady, and pray for us: turn our sadness into joy.

Enlighten me, O Star of the sea: shed thy brightness upon me, O resplendent Virgin.

Extinguish the burning of my heart: refresh me with thy grace.

Let thy grace ever protect me: let thy presence give light to my end.

Glory be to the Father, etc.

PSALM 67

Let Mary arise, and let her enemies be scattered: let them all be crushed beneath her feet.

Break thou the attack of our enemies: destroy all their iniquity.

To thee, O Lady, have I cried in my tribulation: and thou hast given serenity to my conscience.

Let not thy praise fail in our mouths: nor thy love in our hearts.

There is much peace to them that love thee, O Lady: their souls shall not see death forever.

Glory be to the Father, etc.

PSALM 68

Save me, O Lady: for the waters of concupiscence have entered into my very soul.

I am stuck fast in the mire of sin: and the waters of pleasure have encompassed me.

Weeping, I have wept in the night: and the day of joy has arisen for me.

Save my soul, O Mother of the Saviour: for by thee true salvation was given to the world.

While thou wast overshadowed when the Angel spoke to thee: and becamest pregnant with the Wisdom of the Father.

Glory be to the Father, etc.

PSALM 69

O Lady, come to my assistance: and by the light of thy mercy enlighten me.

Teach us to seek thy goodness: that we may declare thy wonders.

Show forth thy power against our enemies: that thou mayest be praised among the distant nations.

In the flames of thy wrath let them be plunged into hell: and may they who trouble thy servants find perdition.

Have mercy on thy servants, upon whom thy name is invoked: and do not permit them to be straitened in their temptations.

Glory be to the Father, etc.

PSALM 70

In thee, O Lady, have I hoped: let me never be confounded: in thy mercy deliver me and free me.

Because of the multitude of my iniquities: I am vehemently oppressed.

Mine enemies have acted above my head: they have mocked me and derided me day by day.

See, O Lady, how I am troubled: stretch forth thy hands, and succour him who perishes.

Delay not, for the sake of the grace of thy name: and thou shalt become unto me joy and salvation.

Glory be to the Father, etc.

PSALM 71

Give to the King thy judgment, O God: and thy mercy to the Queen, His Mother.

In thy hand are life and salvation: perpetual joy and glorious eternity.

Sprinkle my heart with thy sweetness: make me forget the miseries of this life.

Draw me after thee by the bands of thy mercy: and with the bandages of thy grace and loving kindness heal my pain.

Stir up in me a desire for Heaven: and inebriate my soul with the joy of Paradise.

Glory be to the Father, etc.

PSALM 72

How good is God to Israel: to those who pay homage to His Mother and venerate her.

For she is our comfort: she is the most excellent of help in labour.

The enemy hath overspread my soul with darkness: O Lady, make light arise within me.

Let the wrath of God be turned away from me by thee: placate him by thy merits and thy prayers.

Stand for me in the day of judgment: in His presence take up my cause, and be my advocate.

Glory be to the Father, etc.

PSALM 73

O Lady, why hast thou cast us off? and why wilt thou not help us in the day of tribulation?

Let my prayer come into thy sight: and despise not the voices of those who groan.

The enemy hath stretched his bow against us: he has strengthened his right hand, and there is no consoler.

Break for us the bonds of his malicious doings: and deliver us by thy right hand.

Drive him back into the place of perdition: let eternal damnation possess him.

Glory be to the Father, etc.

PSALM 74

We will praise thee, O Lady: and we will praise thy name: make us to delight in thy praises.

Sing ye to her, ye dwellers upon earth: and announce her praise to the peoples.

Praise and magnificence are before her: fortitude and exultation are in her throne.

Adore ye her in her beauty: glorify the Maker of her beauty.

Be mindful in eternity of her mercy: keep in mind her virtues and her wonders.

Glory be to the Father, etc.

PSALM 75

In Judea God is known: in Israel the honour of His Mother.

Sweet is the memory of her above honey and the honeycomb: and her love is above all aromatic perfumes.

Health and life are in her house: and in her dwelling are peace and eternal glory.

Honour her, ye heavens and earth: because the supreme artificer has wonderfully honoured her.

Give to her praise, all ye creatures: and joyfully celebrate her astonishing mercy.

Glory be to the Father, etc.

PSALM 76

With my voice I cried to the Lady: and by her grace she bowed down to me.

She hath taken sorrow and grief from my heart: and she hath soothed my heart by her sweetness.

She hath turned my fear into a sweet confidence: and by her honey-flowing aspect she hath calmed my mind.

By her holy help I have avoided the dangers of death: and I have escaped the cruel hand.

Thanks be to God and to thee, O loving Mother, for all things which I have obtained: for thy piety and thy mercy.

Glory be to the Father, etc.

PSALM 77

Attend, O people of God, to His commandments: and forget not the Queen of grace.

Open your heart to search her out: and your lips to glorify her.

Let her love come down into your hearts: long to please her.

Her beauty outshines the sun and the moon: she is adorned with the ornaments of virtues.

Have mercy on me, O Queen of glory and honour: and keep my soul from all danger.

Glory be to the Father, etc.

PSALM 78

O Lady, the heathen have come into the inheritance of God: which thou hast established in Christ by thy merits.

Let thy speech be sweet before Him: and unite me to Him who hath redeemed me.

Stretch forth thine arm against the cruel enemy: and unfold to me his craft.

Thy voice is sweet above every melody: the angelic harmony cannot be compared with it.

Drop down on me the sweetness of thy graces: and the fragrance of thy heavenly gifts.

Glory be to the Father, etc.

PSALM 79

Give ear to me, thou who rulest Israel: praise thy Mother with me.

Arise and shake thyself from the dust, O my soul: go forth to meet the Queen of Heaven.

Loose the bands of thy neck, O poor little soul of mine: and welcome her with glorious praises.

The odour of life comes forth from her: and all salvation springs out of her heart.

By the sweet fragrance of her spiritual gifts: dead souls are raised to life.

Glory be to the Father, etc.

PSALM 80

Rejoice to the Lady, our helper: sing aloud in the joy of your heart.

Let your affections be enkindled in her: and she will overwhelm your enemies with confusion.

Let us imitate her humility: her obedience and her meekness.

All graces shine forth in her: for her capacity was immense.

Run ye to her with holy devotion: and she will share her good things with you.

Glory be to the Father, etc.

PSALM 81

God is in the congregation of Jews: from whom, as a rose, has come forth the Mother of God.

Wipe away my stains, O Lady: thou who art ever resplendent in purity.

Make the fountain of life flow into my mouth:

whence the living waters take their rise and flow forth.

All ye who thirst, come to her: she will willingly give you to drink from her fountain.

He who drinketh from her, will spring forth unto life everlasting: and he will never thirst.

Glory be to the Father, etc.

PSALM 82

O my Lady, who shall be like unto thee? In grace and glory thou surpassest all.

As the heavens are above the earth: so art thou high above all, and exceedingly exalted.

Wound my heart with thy charity: make me worthy of thy grace and thy gifts.

May my heart melt in thy fear: and may the desire of thee enkindle my soul.

Make me desire thy honour and thy glory: that I may be received by thee into the peace of Jesus Christ.

Glory be to the Father, etc.

PSALM 83

How lovely are thy tabernacles, O Lady of hosts: how delightful are the tents of thy redemption.

Honour her, O ye sinners: and she will obtain grace and salvation for you.

Her prayer is incense above frank-incense and balsam: her supplications will not return to her bare, void, or empty.

Intercede for me, O Lady, with thy Christ: neither do thou forsake me in death or in life.

For thy spirit is kind: thy grace fills the whole world.

Glory be to the Father, etc.

PSALM 84

O Lady, thou hast blessed thy house: thou hast consecrated thy dwelling.

This one is fair among the daughters of Jerusalem: whose memory is in blessing.

The holy angels have proclaimed her blessed: glorify her, ye Virtues and Dominations.

Ye peoples and nations, seek out her prudence: and search out the treasures of her mercy.

Think of her in goodness: and seek her in simplicity of heart.

Glory be to the Father, etc.

PSALM 85

Incline thine ear, O Lady, and hear me: turn thy face to me, and have mercy on me.

May the inflowing of thy sweetness delight the souls of the saints: and the infusion of thy charity be sweet above the sweetest honey.

The resplendence of thy glory enlightens the mind: and the light of thy mercies leads to salvation.

The fountain of thy goodness inebriates the thirsty: and the aspect of thy countenance draws men away from sin.

To know thee and to learn thee is the root of immortality: and to declare thy virtues is the way of salvation.

Glory be to the Father, etc.

PSALM 86

The foundations of life in the soul of the just: are to persevere in charity unto the end.

Thy grace raises up the poor man in adversity: and the invocation of thy name inspires him with confidence.

Paradise is filled with thy tender mercies: and by the fear of thee the infernal enemy is confounded.

He who hopes in thee, will find treasures of peace: and he who invokes thee not in this life, will not attain to the kingdom of God.

Grant, O Lady, that we may live in the grace of the Holy Ghost: and lead our souls to a holy end.

Glory be to the Father, etc.

PSALM 87

Lady, thou art the helper of my salvation: by day and by night I have cried to thee.

Let my prayer enter into thy sight: console my sadness with the sight of thee.

Evils are multiplied in my soul: cleanse it from filth and sin.

May thy power overcome our enemies: lest they hinder our salvation.

Bestow on us thy grace to resist them: strengthen our hearts against the concupiscence of the flesh.

Glory be to the Father, etc.

PSALM 88

Thy mercies, O Lady, I will sing forever.

With the ointment of thy tender mercy heal the broken in heart: and with the oil of thy mercy console our griefs.

May thy gracious countenance appear to me in my end: may the beauty of thy face rejoice my spirit in its going forth.

Stir up my spirit to love thy goodness: excite my mind to extol thy nobility and worth.

Deliver me from evil and tribulation: and from all sin keep thou my soul.

Glory be to the Father, etc.

PSALM 89

O Lady, thou art made unto us refreshment: in all our needs.

The diffusion of thy grace produces thy holy operations in us: and the gentle dropping of thy sweetness maketh holy affections.

I will be mindful, O Lady, of thy tender mercies: I will sing unto thee a sacrifice of praise and a song of joy.

They who honour thee will obtain a perennial crown for ashes: and the mantle of praise for the spirit of mourning.

They who hope in thee will be clothed with light: joy and perpetual rejoicing will be their lot.

Glory be to the Father, etc.

PSALM 90

He that dwelleth in the help of the Mother of God: will abide under her protection.

The concourse of enemies will not harm him: the flying arrow will not touch him.

For she will deliver him from the snare of the hunter: and under her wings she will protect him.

Cry out to her in your dangers: and the scourge will not come nigh your dwelling.

He who has placed his hope in her, will find the fruit of grace: the gate of paradise will be opened to him.

Glory be to the Father, etc.

PSALM 91

It is good to give praise to the Virgin Mary: and to sing glory to her is the prosperity of the mind.

To declare her merits rejoices the mind: and to imitate her works makes glad the angels of God.

He who obtains her favour: is recognised by the dwellers in Paradise.

And he who shall bear the character of her name, shall be written in the book of life.

Arise, O Lady, and judge our cause: and deliver us from those who rise up against us.

Withdraw not thy right hand from the sinner: and meet with thy sword the darts of the destroyer.

Glory be to the Father, etc.

PSALM 92

The Lord hath reigned, He is clothed with beauty: He hath crowned His Mother with the ornaments of virtues.

May the Mother of peace fulfil in us his propitiation: and may she teach her servants the way of equity.

Ye who desire the wisdom of Christ: serve His Mother with a reverent soul.

Who will suffice to relate thy works, O Lady? and who shall search out the treasures of thy mercy?

Do thou uphold those who are fainting away in their temptations: and appoint them a lot in truth.

Glory be to the Father, etc.

PSALM 93

The Lord is a God to whom revenge belongeth: but thou, O Mother of mercy, inclinest Him to mercy.

Thy magnificence, O Lady, is preached forever: and they who venerate thee shall find the way of peace.

Serve her reverently with rejoicing: and the Most Blessed Fruit of her womb shall heal you.

Look, O Lady, upon the humility of thy servants: and they shall praise thee in the generations of ages.

Magnify thy name in the multiplication of thy graces: and permit not thy servants to be subject to perils.

Glory be to the Father, etc.

PSALM 94

Come, let us rejoice to Our Lady: let us joyfully sing to the saving Mary, our Queen.

Let us come before her presence with joy: and in canticles let us all praise her together.

Come, let us adore, and fall down before her: let us confess our sins to her with tears.

Obtain for us a full pardon: stand for us before the tribunal of God.

Receive our souls at our end: and lead us into eternal rest.

Glory be to the Father, etc.

PSALM 95

Sing a new song to her who is full of grace: sing to Mary all ye of the earthly world.

For she excels in sanctity all the angels: and those born of women in her wonders and miracles.

Beauty and glory are in her countenance: and grace is in her eyes.

Bring ye to her glory, ye fathers of the peoples: rejoice in her, all ye creatures of God.

You have an admirable exchange worked by her means: by reason of which you are called the sons of the Most High God.

Glory be to the Father, etc.

PSALM 96

The Lord hath reigned, let Mary rejoice: in all the empire under her rule.

Adore her, all ye citizens of the heavenly commonwealth: exalt her, ye fair virgins, her daughters.

For she is raised above principalities and dominations: she is exalted above angels and the embassies of archangels.

Patriarchs and prophets, break forth in her praise: make a harmony, Apostles and martyrs of Christ.

Confessors and virgins, sing canticles to her from the songs of Sion: and congratulate her, holy monks, for the triumphs she has won.

Glory be to the Father, etc.

PSALM 97

Sing to Our Lady a new song: for she hath done wonderful things.

In the sight of nations she hath revealed her mercy: her name is heard even to the ends of the earth.

Be mindful, O Lady, of the poor and the wretched: and support them by the help of thy holy refreshment.

For thou, O Lady, art sweet and true: exceedingly patient and full of compassion.

Tread upon the enemies of our souls: and crush with thy holy arm their contumacy.

Glory be to the Father, etc.

PSALM 98

The Lord hath reigned, let the people be angry: Mary sits at the right hand under the Cherubim.

Great in Sion is thy glory, O Lady: and in Jerusalem thy magnificence.

Sing before her, ye virginal choirs: and adore her throne, for it is holy.

In her right hand is the fiery law: and round about her are millions of saints.

Her commands are before his eyes: and the rule of justice is in her heart.

Glory be to the Father, etc.

PSALM 99

Sing with joy to Our Lady, ye men of the earth: serve her in joy and pleasantness.

With all your soul draw nigh unto her: and in all your strength keep her ways.

Search her out, and she will be manifested to you: be clean of heart, and you will take hold of her.

To them whom thou shalt help, O Lady, will be the refreshment of peace: and they from whom thou turnest away thy face shall have no hope of salvation.

Be mindful of us, O Lady, and let evil not take hold of us: help us in the end, and we shall find eternal life.

Glory be to the Father, etc.

PSALM 100

To thee, O Lady, will I sing mercy and judgment: I will sing to thee in joy of heart, when thou shalt have made my soul glad.

I will praise thee and thy glory: and thou shalt bestow refreshment upon my soul.

I have been zealous for thy love and thy honour: therefore wilt thou defend my cause before the judge of ages.

I am drawn by thy goodness and grace: I pray thee, let me not be defrauded of my hope and good confidence.

Strengthen thou my soul in my last days: and in this my flesh make me to behold my Saviour.

Glory be to the Father, etc.

PSALM 101

O Lady, hear my prayer: and let my cry come unto thee.

Turn not thy sacred countenance away from me: nor hate me because of my uncleanness.

Forsake me not in the thought and counsel of mine enemies: and permit me not to fall in their wicked attacks.

Those who trust in thee, will not fear the tortuous snake: and those who exalt thee in praises will escape the hand of Acheron.

By thy virginal conception give me a good confidence in thee: and by thy admirable delivery rejoice my soul.

Glory be to the Father, etc.

PSALM 102

Bless, O my soul, the Mother of Jesus Christ: and all that is within me, glorify her name.

Forget not her benefits: nor her grace and consolation.

By her grace sins are forgiven: and by her mercy maladies are healed.

Bless her, all ye powers of Heaven: glorify her, ye choirs of the Apostles and Prophets.

Bless her, O ye sea, and the islands of the nations: sing a hymn to her, all ye heavens and the dwellers therein.

Glory be to the Father, etc.

PSALM 103

Bless, O my soul, the Virgin Mary: her honour and her magnificence forever.

Thou hast clothed thyself with beauty and comeliness: thou art clad, O Lady, with a shining garment.

From thee proceeds the healing of sins: and the discipline of peace, and the fervour of charity.

Fill us, thy servants, with holy virtues: and let the wrath of God not come nigh unto us.

Give eternal joy to thy servants: and forget them not in the death struggle.

Glory be to the Father, etc.

PSALM 104

Give praise to Our Lady and call upon her name: sing gloriously unto her, declaring her virtues.

Praise and exalt her, O Virgins, daughters of Sion: because she will espouse to you the King of Angels.

Honour ye the Queen full of all grace: and contemplate with reverence her most holy countenance.

Eternal salvation is in thy hand, O Lady: those who honour thee worthily will receive it.

Thy clemency will not fail in the eternal years: and thy mercy is from generation to generation.

Glory be to the Father, etc.

PSALM 105

Give praise to Our Lady, for she is good: in all the tribes of the earth relate her mercies.

Far from the impious is her conversation: her foot has not declined from the way of the Most High.

A fountain of fertilising grace comes forth from her mouth: and a virginal emanation sanctifying chaste souls.

The hope of the glory of Paradise is in her heart: for the devout soul who shall have honoured her.

Have mercy on us, O resplendent Queen of Heaven: and give consolation from thy glory.

Glory be to the Father, etc.

PSALM 106

Give praise to the Lord, for He is good: give praise to His Mother, for her mercy endureth for ever.

Show us, O Lady, the innocence and the way of prudence: and point out the way of understanding to thy servants.

The fear of God enlightens the mind: and thy love rejoices it.

Blessed is the man whose speech is pleasing to thee: his bones shall be fattened with marrow and fatness.

Thy word shall uphold the feeble soul: and thy lips shall refresh the thirsty soul.

Glory be to the Father, etc.

PSALM 107

My heart is ready, O Lady, my heart is ready: to sing praises to thee and to chant.

Greater is thy love than all riches: and thy grace is above gold and precious stones.

Beatitude and justice are given by God: for those who turn away from their sins to thee shall obtain the remedy of penance.

Thy fruits are grace and peace: and those who please thee shall be far from perdition.

Be to us a shade of protection in our temptations:

let the spreading of thy wings defend us from him who devours.

Glory be to the Father, etc.

PSALM 108

O Lady, despise not my praise: and deign to accept this Psalter dedicated to thee.

Look upon the will of my heart: and make my affection well-pleasing to thee.

Hasten to visit thy servants: under the protection of thy hand may they be preserved unhurt.

May they receive through thee the illumination of the Holy Spirit: and refreshment against the heat of cupidity.

Heal, O Lady, the contrite of heart: and revive them by the ointment of piety.

Glory be to the Father, etc.

PSALM 109

The Lord said to Our Lady: Sit at my right hand, O my Mother!

Goodness and sanctity have pleased thee: therefore thou shalt reign with me forever.

The crown of immortality is on thy holy head: whose brightness and glory shall not be extinguished.

Have mercy on us, O Lady, mother of light and splendour: enlighten us, O Lady of truth and virtue.

From thy treasures pour into us the wisdom of God: and the understanding of prudence, and the model of discipline.

Glory be to the Father, etc.

PSALM 110

I will give praise to thee, O Lady, with my whole soul: I will glorify thee with my whole mind.

The works of thy grace will remain: and the testament of thy mercy before the throne of God.

By thee redemption has been sent from God: the repentant people shall have the hope of salvation.

A good understanding to all who honour thee: and their lot is among the angels of peace.

Glorious and admirable is thy name: those who keep it will not fear in the moment of death.

Glory be to the Father, etc.

PSALM 111

Blessed is the man who feareth the Lady: and blessed is the heart that loves her.

Happy the man who is never satiated with thy praise: and grows not weary of the narration of thy virtues.

In his heart has arisen the light of God: the Holy Spirit enlightens his understanding.

Bestow, O Lady, thy grace upon thy poor: revive the hungry and the needy.

By thee names shall be in eternal remembrance: our heart shall not fear the evil hearing.

Glory be to the Father, etc.

PSALM 112

Praise, ye children, the Mother of God: ye old men, glorify her name.

Blessed be Mary, the Mother of Christ: for she is the way to the homeland of sanctity.

Her throne is high above the Cherubim: her throne is above the hinges of heaven.

Her countenance is upon the humble: and her looks upon those who trust in her.

Her mercy is over all flesh: and her almsgiving until the ends of the earth.

Glory be to the Father, etc.

PSALM 113

In the going forth of my soul from this world: meet it, O Lady, and receive it.

Console it with thy holy countenance: let not the sight of the demons terrify it.

Be to it a ladder to Heaven: and a straight way to the Paradise of God.

Obtain for it from the Father the pardon of peace: and a throne of light among the servants of God.

Uphold the devout before the tribunal of Christ: take their cause into thy hands.

Glory be to the Father, etc.

PSALM 114

I have loved the Mother of the Lord my God: and the light of her compassions she hath shined upon me.

The sorrows of death have encompassed me: and the visitation of Mary hath rejoiced me.

I have incurred grief and danger: and I have been recreated by her grace.

Let her name and her memory be in the midst of our heart: and the blow of the malignant will not injure us.

Be converted, my soul, unto her praise: and thou shalt find refreshment in thy last end.

Glory be to the Father, etc.

PSALM 115

I believed, therefore I have spoken: thy glory, O Lady, to the whole world.

Have compassion on my soul, and guide it: deign in thy good pleasure to take possession of it.

Assign to it the testament of thy peace and thy love: give to it the memory of thy name.

Of the blessing of thy womb give me support:

and from the fatness of thy grace sweeten my soul.

Break thou the bonds of my sins: and with thy virtues adorn the face of my soul.

Glory be to the Father, etc.

PSALM 116

Praise ye our Lady, all ye nations: glorify her, all ye peoples.

For her grace and her mercy are confirmed upon us: and her truth remaineth forever.

He who shall worthily have venerated her, will be justified: but he who shall have neglected her, will die in his sins.

The lips of angels shall relate her wisdom: and all the citizens of Paradise will sing her praises.

Those who approach her with a good soul: will not be seized by the devastating angel.

Glory be to the Father, etc.

PSALM 117

Give praise to the Lord, for He is good: give praise to His Mother, for her mercy endureth forever.

The love of her driveth out sin from the heart: and her grace purifieth the conscience of the sinner.

The way to come to Christ is to approach her: he who shall fly her shall not find the way of peace.

Let him who is hardened in sins, often call upon her: and light shall arise in his darkness.

He who is sad in his heart, let him cry out to her: and he will be inebriated with a sweet-flowing dew.

Glory be to the Father, etc.

PSALM 118

Blessed are the undefiled in the way: who imitate the Mother of God.

Blessed are the imitators of her humility: blessed are the sharers in her charity.

Blessed are the searchers into her virtues: blessed are they who are conformed to her image.

Blessed are they who venerate her conception and her birth: blessed are they who devoutly serve her.

Blessed are they who have hope and confidence in her: blessed are they who receive through her eternal happiness.

Glory be to the Father, etc.

PSALM 118A

Give bountifully to thy servant, O Lady: enliven me, and I shall do thy will.

I am a sojourner on the earth: hide nothing of thy love from me.

My soul hath longed to desire thy praise: at all times.

For thou art my salvation in the Lord: who hast delivered me, one condemned to death.

What shall I give back for these things, except my whole self? O Lady receive me.

Glory be to the Father, etc.

PSALM 118B

Set before me for a law, O Lady, the holy of holies of thy will: and I shall always seek after it.

Lead me into the path of thy tender mercies, O most beautiful of women: for this same have I desired.

Incline my soul to the love of those above, O Lady: and not to unchasteness.

Behold I have coveted thy chastity from my youth up: in thy mercy strengthen me.

And I will keep the way of thy testimonies forever: and I will search out the commandments of thy Son, which I have loved.

Glory be to the Father, etc.

PSALM 118C

Be mindful of thy word, O Princess of all ladies: in which thou hast given me hope.

In the stormy waves of tempests it hath powerfully held me: for thy word hath quickened me.

Lying men have surrounded me, and scourges are

gathered together upon me: and behold thy hand hath delivered me.

I have communicated all good things to them that fear thee: and to those who earnestly kept thy commandments.

The earth is full of thy tender mercies: therefore, have I sought out the way of thy justifications.

Glory be to the Father, etc.

PSALM 118D

Thou hast done well with thy servant, O Lady: and because of this the angels rejoice.

Teach me the discipline of thy manners and thy equity: because I have believed in thy words above all others.

It is good for me that with thy burden thou hast humbled me: that I may follow thy conversation.

Those who love thy servants, shall be venerated: but he who shall hate them, will fall in eternity.

Let the drops of thy clemency ever fall upon me from above, and I shall live: for thy holy law is my meditation.

Glory be to the Father, etc.

PSALM 118E

My soul hath fainted in thy ways, O Lady: and unless thou didst have the greatest compassion on me, I should indeed have perished in my weakness.

My eyes have failed in thy contemplation: like a bottle in the frost my soul has been before thee.

According to thy goodness quicken thou me: and I shall not forget thy words, because to cling to thee is good.

By thy ruling the world goes on: which thou together with God hast founded from the beginning.

I am all thine, O Lady; save me: for thy praises were desirable to me in the time of my pilgrimage.

Glory be to the Father, etc.

PSALM 118F

How have I loved thy law, O Lady: it is forever in my sight.

The abundance of thy sweetnesses has drawn my heart out of me: and my flesh hath wonderfully rejoiced in thee.

How sweet to sinners are thy words, O Lady: above all melody thy refection is sweet to my mouth.

Thy word is a light to my steps: and an ineffable illumination to my paths.

How often have sinners of hell exasperated me, because I would not stray from thy charity: but in thee, O Lady have I hoped.

Glory be to the Father, etc.

PSALM 118G

I have hated the unjust: and I have loved thy way, O gracious Lady.

Help me, O Lady of the world, and I shall be saved: and I shall meditate the honour of thy commandments.

Make me always stand in thy fear: and deliver me not up, O Virgin, to those who calumniate me.

I am of thy own tongue: I am the least in thy family.

Keep me, O Lady, from those who neglect the judgments of thy justice.

Thou despisest all who depart from thy service: because their thought is unjust.

Glory be to the Father, etc.

PSALM 118H

Wonderful are thy testimonies, O kind Mother: and by thy words my heart is enlightened.

All the rich of the people shall entreat thy countenance: and the daughters of kings shall praise thy face.

The word of thy lips is burning exceedingly: He who shall make haste to come to thee, shall share in it.

I am as a trembling reed before thee: hold me, Lady, under thy yoke, and I shall not be confounded.

The dragons of hell attack thy servants above all others: but do thou, O Lady, defend us.

Glory be to the Father, etc.

PSALM 118 I

I have cried out to thee with my whole heart, O Lady: mercifully deliver me from my necessities.

Hear the voice of my groaning, O my Lady: teach me what is acceptable to thee at all times.

Salvation is far from those who know thee not: but he who perseveres in thy service is far from perdition.

Thy mercy rules all things: O Lady, in thy salvation quicken me.

The beginning of thy words is truth at all times: and I have not forgotten thine immaculate law.

Glory be to the Father, etc.

PSALM 118 J

Princes have persecuted me without cause: and the wicked spirit fears the invocation of thy name.

There is much peace to them that keep thy name, O Mother of God: and to them there is no stumbling-block.

At the seven hours I have sung praises to thee, O Lady: according to thy word give me understanding.

Let my prayer come into thy sight, that I may

not forsake thee, O Lady, all the days of my life: for thy ways are mercy and truth.

I will long forever to praise thee, O Lady: when thou shalt have taught me thy justifications.

Glory be to the Father, etc.

PSALM 119

I cried to Our Lady when I was in trouble: and she heard me.

Lady, deliver us from all evil: all the days of our life.

Crush the head of our enemies: with the insuperable power of thy foot.

As thy spirit hath rejoiced in God thy Saviour: so do thou deign to pour true joy into my heart.

Approach to Our Lord to pray for us: that by thee our sins may be blotted out.

Glory be to the Father, etc.

PSALM 120

To thee I have raised mine eyes, O Mother of Christ: by whom comfort cometh to all flesh.

Bestow on us thy help and thy grace: in all our tribulations.

Keep us, O Lady: lest we be caught in the snare of sinners.

The pupil of thine eye neither slumbers nor sleeps: that we may always be kept under thy protection.

The tongues of men and angels praise thee: and before thee every knee shall bow.

Glory be to the Father, etc.

PSALM 121

I rejoiced in thee, O Queen of Heaven: because under thy leadership we shall go into the house of the Lord.

Jerusalem the heavenly city: may we attain to the rewards of Mary.

Obtain for us, O Lady, peace and pardon: and the victory over our enemies, and triumph. ,

Strengthen and console our hearts: by the sweetness of thy piety.

So, Lady, pour into us thy mercy: that we may devoutly die in the Lord.

Glory be to the Father, etc.

PSALM 122

To thee have I raised up mine eyes, O Queen: who reignest in Heaven.

Let our help be in the power of thy name: let all our works be directed by thee.

Blessed be thou in Heaven and on earth: in the sea and in all abysses.

Blessed be thy fecundity: blessed be thy virginity and purity.

Blessed be thy holy body: blessed be thy most holy soul.

Glory be to the Father, etc.

PSALM 123

Unless our Lady was in us: many dangers would have overtaken us.

O Virgin, be our defender: and a propitious advocate before God.

Show us, O Lady, thy mercy: and strengthen us in thy holy service.

Let the holy angels bless thee in Heaven: let all men bless thee upon earth.

Give not up to the beasts the souls of them that trust in thee: let not the mouths of them that sing to thee be closed.

Glory be to the Father, etc.

PSALM 124

Those who trust in thee, O Mother of God: shall not fear at the face of the enemy.

Rejoice and exult, all ye who love her: because she will help you in the day of your trouble.

Be mindful of thy tender mercies, O Lady: and relieve us in the pilgrimage of our sojourning.

Turn thine amiable countenance towards us: confound and destroy all our enemies.

Blessed be all the works of thy hands, O Lady: blessed be all thy holy miracles.

Glory be to the Father, etc.

PSALM 125

When thou shalt turn thy most serene countenance upon us: thou shalt rejoice us, O virginal Mother of God.

Blessed be thou, O treasury of Christ: above all women upon earth.

Blessed be thy glorious name: which the mouth of the Lord hath wonderfully named.

Let not thy praise fail from our lips: nor thy charity from our hearts.

Those who love thee will be blessed by God: and those who wish to love thee, will not be defrauded of their confidence.

Glory be to the Father, etc.

PSALM 126

Unless, O Lady, thou shalt build the house of our heart: its edifice shall not remain.

Build us up by thy grace and thy power: that we may remain firm forever.

Blessed be thy word: and blessed be all the words of thy lips.

Let them be blessed by God, who shall bless thee:

and let them be reckoned in the number of the just.

Bless, O Lady, them that bless thee: and never turn thy gracious countenance away from them.

Glory be to the Father, etc.

PSALM 127

Blessed are all they who fear our Lady: and blessed are all they who know how to do thy will and thy good pleasure.

Blessed are the father and mother who have begotten thee: whose memory shall abide forever.

Blessed is the womb that bore thee: and blessed are the breasts that nourished thee.

Turn thou thy mercy toward us: and be gracious to thy servants.

Look upon us and behold our shame: take away from us all our iniquities.

Glory be to the Father, etc.

PSALM 128

My enemies have often troubled me from my youth up: deliver me, O Lady, and vindicate my cause from them.

Give them not power over my soul: keep my interior and my exterior.

Obtain for us pardon for our sins: let it be given to us by the grace of the Holy Spirit.

Make us do penance worthily and praiseworthily: that we may come to God by a blessed end.

Show us then with a gracious and serene countenance: the glorious fruit of thy womb.

Glory be to the Father, etc.

PSALM 129

Out of the depths I have cried to thee, O Lady: Lady, hear my prayer.

Let thine ears be attentive: to the voice of praise and of thy glorification.

Deliver me from the hand of my adversaries: confound their plans and their attempts against me.

Deliver me in the evil day: and in the day of death forget not my soul.

Lead me unto the harbour of salvation: may my name be written among the just.

Glory be to the Father, etc.

PSALM 130

Lady, my heart hath not been exalted: nor have mine eyes been lifted up.

The Lord hath blessed thee in His power: who by thee hath reduced to naught our enemies.

Blessed be He who hath sanctified thee: and who hath brought thee forth pure from thy mother's womb.

Blessed be He who hath overshadowed thee: and by His grace hath given thee fecundity.

Bless us, O Lady, and strengthen us in thy grace: that by thee we may be presented before the sight of the Lord.

Glory be to the Father, etc.

PSALM 131

Be mindful, O Lady, of David: and of all who invoke thy name.

Give us confidence in thy name: and let our adversaries be confounded.

Console us in the land of our pilgrimage: and relieve our poverty.

Give us, O holy Virgin, the bread of tears: and sorrow for our sins in the land of our sojourning.

Make the Blessed Fruit of thy womb propitious to us: that we may be filled with the grace of the Holy Spirit.

Glory be to the Father, etc.

PSALM 132

Behold how good and how pleasant, O Mary, it is: to love thy name.

Thy name is as oil poured out, and as an aromatic fragrance: to those who love it.

How great is the multitude of thy sweetness, O

Lady: which thou hast prepared for those who love and hope in thee.

Be a refuge to the poor in tribulation: because thou art a staff to the poor and wretched.

Let them, I beseech thee, find grace with God: who invoke thy help in their needs.

Glory be to the Father, etc.

PSALM 133

Behold now, bless ye the Lady: all ye who hope in her holy name.

Rejoice with a great joy, you who exalt and glorify her: because you will be rejoiced by the plentifulness of her consolations.

Behold now with an overflowing bounty she will come down upon you: to console and to make glad your hearts.

Bless her, all her servants: and let her memory be the desire of your soul.

Bless her, all ye angels and saints of God: praise her wonders forever.

Glory be to the Father, etc.

PSALM 134

Praise the name of the Lord: bless the name of Mary, His Mother.

Be diligent in prayer to Mary: and she will raise up for you eternal delights.

Let us come to her in a contrite soul: and sinful cupidity will not besiege us.

He who thinks of her in tranquillity of mind: shall find sweetness and the rest of peace.

Let us breathe forth our souls to her in our end: and she will lay open to us the courts of them that triumph.

Glory be to the Father, etc.

PSALM 135

Give praise to the Lord, for He is good: because by His most sweet Mother, the Virgin Mary, mercy is given to us.

Obtain for us, O Lady, the friendship of Jesus Christ: and keep us lest we should lose our innocence.

Repress our enemy by thy command: lest he should destroy in us the virtue of charity.

Illumine our ways and our paths: that we may know what is pleasing to God.

Preserve in us what is naturally good: and may good graces be multiplied in us.

Glory be to the Father, etc.

PSALM 136

On the rivers of Babylon the Hebrews wept: but let us weep over our sins.

Let us cry out humbly to the Virgin and Mother: let us offer her our plaints and our sighs.

There is no propitiation to be found without her: nor salvation apart from her fruit.

By her, sins are purged away: and by her fruit, souls are made white.

By her is made satisfaction for sins; by her fruit health is bestowed.

Glory be to the Father, etc.

PSALM 137

I will praise thee, O Lady, with my whole heart: because by thee I have experienced the clemency of Jesus Christ.

Hear, O Lady, my words and prayers: and in the sight of angels I will sing praise to thee.

In whatever day thou shalt invoke me, hear me: and multiply thy power in my soul.

Let all tribes and tongues praise thee: because by thee salvation is restored to us.

From all trouble save thy servants: and make them live under thy protection and peace.

Glory be to the Father, etc.

PSALM 138

O Lady, thou hast tried me and known me: my ruin and my transgression.

Thy mercy is plentiful above me: and thy clemency is great to me.

Thine eye hath beheld mine imperfect being: and thine eyebrows have known my ways.

We have from the Holy Spirit an abundance of holy desires: and the stain of sin does not trouble our conscience.

The light of thy mercy makes serene our heart: and the sweetness of thy peace recreates us.

Glory be to the Father, etc.

PSALM 139

Deliver me, O Lady, from all evil: and from the infernal enemy defend me.

Against me he hath drawn his bow: and in his craftiness he hath laid snares for me.

Restrain his evil power: and powerfully crush his craft.

Turn back his iniquity on his own head: and let him speedily fall into the pit which he hath made.

But we will rejoice in thy service: and we will glory in thy praise.

Glory be to the Father, etc.

PSALM 140

O Lady, I have cried to thee, hear me: incline unto my prayer and to my supplication.

Let my supplication be directed as incense before thy face: both in the time of the evening sacrifice and in the morning.

Let not my heart turn aside into spiteful words: and let not the thought of wickedness upset my mind.

Make me submissive to the good pleasure of thy heart: and let me be conformed to thy actions.

With the sword of understanding pierce my heart: and with the dart of charity inflame my mind.

Glory be to the Father, etc.

PSALM 141

With my voice I have cried to Our Lady: I have humbly entreated her.

I have poured out my tears in her sight: and I have set before her my grief.

The enemy lieth in wait for my heel: he has spread his net before me.

Help me, O Lady, lest I fall before him: let him be crushed beneath my feet.

Lead my soul out of prison: that it may praise thee and sing to the mighty God forever.

Glory be to the Father, etc.

PSALM 142

O Lady, hear my prayer: incline thine ear to my supplication.

The spiteful enemy hath persecuted my life: he hath cast on to the ground my ways.

He hath blackened me with his darkness: and my spirit is exceedingly troubled.

Turn not thy face away from me: that I may not fall together with them that tumble into the abyss.

Send forth thy light and thy grace: and repair anew my life and my conscience.

Glory be to the Father, etc.

PSALM 143

Blessed be thou, O Lady, who teachest thy servants to fight: and strengthenest them against the enemy.

With thy lightnings and thy brightness scatter him: send forth thy darts, that thou mayest confound him.

Glorify from on high thy hand: and let thy servants sing thy praise and thy glory.

Raise up from earthly things our affection: from these eternal delights refresh our interior.

Kindle in our hearts the longing for heavenly things: and deign to refresh us with the joys of Paradise.

Glory be to the Father, etc.

PSALM 144

I will exalt thee, O Mother of the Son of God: and every day I will sing thy praises.

Generations and peoples will praise thy works: and the islands shall expect thy mercy.

The angels will utter the abundance of thy sweetness: and the saints will pronounce thy sweetness.

Our eyes hope in thee, O Lady: send us food and delightful nourishment.

My tongue shall speak thy praise: and I will bless thee for ever and ever.

Glory be to the Father, etc.

PSALM 145

My soul, praise Our Lady: I will glorify her as long as I live.

Never cease from her praises: and think of her every moment.

When my spirit shall go forth, Lady, let it be commended to thee: and in the unknown land be thou its guide.

Let not past sins trouble it: nor let it be disturbed by the meeting with the malignant one.

Lead it to the harbour of salvation: there let it await securely the coming of the Redeemer.

Glory be to the Father, etc.

PSALM 146

Praise the Lady, for a psalm is good: let the praise of her be pleasant and beautiful.

For she heals the broken-hearted: and she refreshes them with the ointment of piety.

Great is her power: and her clemency has no end.

Sing to her in jubilation: and in her praise sing a psalm to her.

Those who hope in the Lord are a good pleasure to her: and those who hope in her mercy.

Glory be to the Father, etc.

PSALM 147

Praise, O Jerusalem, Our Lady: glorify her also, O Sion.

For she buildeth up thy walls: and blesseth thy sons.

Let her grace nourish thee: let her give peace to thy borders.

The Most High hath sent forth His Word: and His power hath overshadowed her.

Let us raise our hearts and hands up to her: that we may feel her influence.

Glory be to the Father, etc.

PSALM 148

Let us praise Our Lady in the heavens: glorify her in the highest.

Praise her, all ye men and beasts: birds of the air, and fishes of the sea.

Praise her, sun and moon: stars, and the orbs of the planets.

Praise her, Cherubim and Seraphim: thrones and dominations and powers.

Praise her, all ye legions of angels: praise her all order of heavenly dwellers.

Glory be to the Father, etc.

PSALM 149

Sing a new song to Our Lady: her praise in the congregation of the just.

Let the heavens rejoice in her glory: the isles of the sea and the whole world.

Fire and water praise her: cold and heat, splendour and light.

Let her praises be in the mouth of the just: and her glory in the band of the triumphant.

City of God, be joyful in her: and for thy dwellers sing her a constant song.

Glory be to the Father, etc.

PSALM 150

Praise Our Lady in her saints: praise her in her virtues and miracles.

Praise her, ye bands of Apostles: praise her, ye choirs and patriarchs and prophets.

Praise her, ye army of martyrs; praise her, ye bands of doctors and confessors.

Praise her in the college of virgins and the chaste: praise her, ye orders of monks and holy anchorites.

Praise her, ye monasteries of all religious: praise her, all the souls of all heavenly dwellers. Let every spirit praise Our Lady!

Glory be to the Father, etc.

CANTICLES IN HONOR OF MARY

A CANTICLE ON THE MODEL OF ISAIAS (XII)

I will praise thee, O Lady, because by thee the Lord has been rendered favourable unto me: and has consoled me.

Behold, Lady, thou art my saviour: I will deal confidently in thee, and will not be confounded.

For thou art my strength and my praise in the Lord: and thou hast become salvation unto me.

I will draw waters in joy from the rivulet: and I will always invoke thy name.

Make known among the peoples the virtues of Our Lady: for her name is exceedingly sublime.

Exalt her and praise her, all the human race: because the Lord my God has given to thee such a mediatrix.

Glory be to the Father, etc.

A CANTICLE LIKE THAT OF EZECHIAS (IS. XXXVIII)

I have said in the midst of my days: I will go to Mary, that she may reconcile me to Christ.

I have sought the residue of my years: in the bitterness of my soul.

My generation is taken away: because my father and mother and all have forsaken me: but Mary hath taken me up.

I hoped in her in the morning, in the evening, and at midday: as a lion she hath broken all the bones of my sins.

And thou, O Lady, hast delivered my soul, that it should not be lost: and my only one from the hand of the dog.

Glory be to the Father, etc.

A CANTICLE LIKE THAT OF ANNA

My heart has rejoiced in the Lord: and my heart has exalted in my Lady.

For He who is mighty has done great things to me: by Mary His Mother.

There is no one holy as is Our Lady: who alone hath surpassed all.

Let the old things depart from our mouth: and let us speak with new tongues.

Exalt and praise Mary, O Sion and Jerusalem: for she is great amongst the ladies of Israel.

She makes poor and she enriches: she humbles and she exalts.

She is higher than the heavens: she is wider than the earth: is this Lady of ours.

Glory be to the Father, etc.

A CANTICLE LIKE THAT OF MARY (EXOD. XV)

Let us sing to Our Lady, the glorious Virgin Mary: let us bless her in hymns and praises.

The name of Our Lady is omnipotent after that of God: she hath cast the chariot of Pharao and his army into the sea.

Thy right hand, O Lady, is magnified in strength: because in the multitude of thy mercies thou hast prostrated mine adversaries.

Thou hast delivered me, O Lady, from the mouth of the lion: and as the mother her new-born infant hast thou received me.

O my most dear Lady: like the hen, cover me with thy wonderful protection.

I am all thine: and all my things are thine, O Virgin blessed above all.

I will place thee as a seal upon my heart: because thy love is strong as death.

Glory be to the Father, etc.

A CANTICLE LIKE HABACUC'S (III)

O Lady, I have heard thy hearing: and I was astonished: I have considered thy works, and I have feared.

Lady, thy work: in the midst of the years thou hast quickened it.

I will praise thee, O Lady: for thou hast hidden these things from the wise, and hast revealed them to little ones.

Thy glory hath covered the heavens: and the earth is full of thy mercy.

Thou hast gone forth, O Virgin, in the salvation of thy people: to their salvation with Christ.

O blessed one, in thy hands is laid up our salvation: be mindful, O loving one, of our poverty.

He whom thou wilt save, will be saved: and he from whom thou shalt turn away thy face, will go down to destruction.

Glory be to the Father, etc.

A CANTICLE LIKE THAT OF MOSES (DEUT. XXXII)

Hear, ye heavens, what I shall speak of Mary: let the earth hear the words of my mouth.

Magnify her together with me: and let us exalt her name forever and ever.

O wicked and perverse generation: acknowledge our Lady for thy salvatrix.

Is she not thy mother, who hath possessed thee: and generated thee in faith?

If thou leavest her, thou art not the friend of the supreme Caesar: for without her He will not save thee.

Would that thou couldst understand, and be wise: and provide for thy last end!

As an infant without a nurse cannot live: so thou canst not have salvation without Our Lady.

Let thy soul thirst for her, hold her, and do not let her go: until she has blessed thee.

Let thy mouth be filled with her praises: sing her magnificence the whole day long.

Glory be to the Father, etc.

A CANTICLE LIKE THAT OF THE THREE CHILDREN

Bless, all works, our glorious Lady: praise and superexalt her forever.

Bless our Lady, ye Angels: ye heavens, bless our Lady.

Let every creature bless our Lady: whom the King wishes thus to be blessed.

Blessed be thou, O daughter of the most High King: who by thy fragrance surpassest all lilies.

Blessed be thou, crown of all ladies: blessed be thou, glory of Jerusalem.

Thy odour is like a full field which the Lord hath blessed: which overflows on those who bless thee, watering their whole souls and minds.

Whosoever shall bless thee, O Blessed Virgin: let him be blessed forever.

He who shall curse thee, O most white rose: let him be accursed.

Let not the abundance of wine and oil: depart from the house of thy servants.

In thy name let every knee bow: in Heaven, on earth, and in hell.

Let us bless God, who hath created thee: blessed be both thy parents who have begotten thee.

Blessed be thou, O Lady, in Heaven and on earth: worthy of praise, and glorious and superexalted forever.

Glory be to the Father, etc.

A CANTICLE LIKE THAT OF ZACHARIAS (LUKE I)

Blessed be thou, O Lady and Mother of my God of Israel: who by thee hath quickened and hath wrought the redemption of His people.

And hath raised up a horn of salvation of thy chastity: in the house of David, His servant.

As he spoke by the mouth of Isaias: and others of his holy prophets.

Give us salvation from our enemies, O Virgin of virgins: from the hand of those who hate us, give us peace.

And do thy mercy for us and our relations: that thou mayest be mindful of the testament of the Almighty God,

Which he hath sworn to our fathers: to Abraham and his seed forever;

That thus, being delivered from the hand of our enemies: we may serve Him in peace.

In sanctity and justice before thee: all our days.

And thou, O Mary, shalt be called the Prophet of God: for thou hast known that He hath regarded the humility of His handmaid.

By whom He hath given the knowledge of salvation to His people: in the remission of their sins.

By the bowels of the multitude of thy mercies: visit us, O Morning Star, the Orient from on high.

Enlighten the darknesses of those who sit in the shadow of death, and deign to instill into them the light of thy most Beloved Son.

Have mercy, O Mother of Mercies, on us miserable sinners, who neglect to do penance for our past sins: and daily commit so much that deserves penance.

Glory be to the Father, etc.

HYMN AFTER THE MODEL OF THE "TE DEUM"

We praise thee, O Mother of God: we confess thee, Mary, ever Virgin.

Thou art the Spouse of the Eternal Father: the whole earth venerates thee.

Thee all angels and archangels, thrones and principalities serve.

Thee all powers and all virtues of Heaven: and all dominations obey.

Before thee all the angelic choirs: the Cherubim and Seraphim exulting stand.

Canticles in Honor of Mary

With unceasing voice every angelic creature proclaims thee:

Holy, holy, holy: Mary, Mother of God and Virgin!

Full are the heavens and the earth: of the majesty and glory of the fruit of thy womb.

Thee the glorious choir of Apostles: praise as the Mother of their Creator.

Thee the white-robed multitude of blessed martyrs: glorify as the Mother of Christ.

Thee the glorious army of Confessors: style the Temple of the Trinity.

Thee the amiable choir of holy virgins: preaches as the example of virginity and humility.

Thee the whole heavenly court: honoureth as Queen.

The Church, invoking thee, calls thee throughout the whole world: Mother of the Divine Majesty.

Venerating thee as the true Mother of the heavenly King: holy, sweet, and loving.

Thou art the Lady of Angels: thou art the gate of Paradise.

Thou art the ladder of glory: and of the heavenly kingdom.

Thou art the bridal chamber: thou art the ark of piety and grace.

Thou art the vein of mercy: thou art the Spouse and the Mother of the Eternal King.

Thou art the temple of the treasury of the

Holy Ghost: thou art the noble throne of the whole blessed Trinity.

Thou art the Mediatrix of God, and the lover of men: the heavenly Illuminatrix of mortal men.

Thou art the inspirer of the warriors, the advocate of the poor: the compassionate refuge of sinners.

Thou art the distributrix of gifts: the barrier against demons and the proud, and their fear.

Thou art the Lady of the world, the Queen of Heaven: after God our only hope.

Thou art the salvation of them that call upon thee: the harbour of the shipwrecked, the solace of the wretched, the refuge of those who perish.

Thou art the Mother of all the blessed, full of joy after God: the comfort of all the dwellers in Heaven.

Thou art the promotrix of the just, the one who gathers together those who stray: the promise of the patriarchs.

Thou art the truth of the prophets, the herald and teacher of the Apostles: the Mistress of the Evangelists.

Thou art the strength of martyrs, the example of confessors: the honour and the festivity of virgins.

Thou hast received into thy womb the Son of God: to deliver exiled man.

By thee is driven out the ancient enemy: and the kingdoms of Heaven are opened to believers.

Thou sittest together with thy Son: at the right hand of the Father.

Do thou intercede for us, O Virgin Mary: with Him who we believe will come to judge us.

We beseech thee, therefore, help us, thy servants: who have been redeemed with the Precious Blood of Thy Son.

Save thy people, O Lady: that we may be partakers of the inheritance of Thy Son.

And rule us: and keep us forever.

Day by day, O loving one: we salute thee.

And we desire to praise thee forever: with both mind and voice.

Deign, O sweet Mary, now and forever: to keep us without sin.

Have mercy on us, O loving one: have mercy on us.

Let thy great mercy be upon us: because we trust in thee, O Virgin Mary.

In thee, O sweet Mary, we hope: do thou defend us forever.

Praise becometh thee; empire is thine: to thee be power and glory forever. Amen.

A MARIAN CREED AFTER THE MANNER OF THAT OF ST. ATHANASIUS

Whoever wishes to be saved, before all must hold a firm faith as to Mary.

Which unless anyone shall keep whole and inviolate: without doubt he shall perish forever.

For she alone, remaining a virgin, hath brought forth: she alone hath destroyed all heresies.

Let the Jew be confounded and ashamed: who says that Christ was born from the seed of Joseph.

Let the Manichean be confounded who says: that Christ has an unreal body.

Let all be ashamed who say: that He derives His Body from any other source than Mary.

For the very same Son, who is the only-begotten of the Father in the Godhead: is the true and only-begotten Son of the Virgin Mary.

In Heaven without a mother: on earth without a father.

For as the rational soul and the flesh because of the union in man is truly born from man: so Christ, both God and Man, is truly begotten by Mary, the Virgin.

Clothing Himself with flesh from the flesh of the Virgin: because so it behooved the human race to be redeemed.

Who according to the Divinity is equal to the Father: but according to His Humanity is less than the Father.

Conceived of the Holy Ghost in the womb of the Virgin Mary, and announced by the Angel: but nevertheless the Holy Spirit is not His Father.

Begotten in the world of the Virgin Mary without pain of the flesh: because He was conceived without carnal delight.

Whom the Mother hath fed with her milk: her breast full of heaven.

Whom the Angels surrounded as attendants at birth: announcing great joy to the shepherds.

He it is who was adored by the Magi with gifts, who fled from Herod into Egypt, who was baptized by John in the Jordan: was betrayed, seized, scourged, crucified, dead, and buried.

Who rose again with glory: and ascended into Heaven.

Who sent the Holy Spirit upon His disciples: and upon His Mother.

Whom He in the end took up into Heaven: where she sitteth at the right hand of her Son, never ceasing to make intercession for us.

This is the faith of the Virgin Mary: which, unless anyone faithfully and firmly believes, he cannot be saved.

THE END

300^2

INDEX

Advantages, Twelve, of the Fruit of the womb of Mary, 185 ff.
Anna, 159
Assumption, 123
Aurora, Mary compared to the, 98 ff.
Axa, 150

Beatitude, Grace of, 58 ff.

Canticles in honor of the Blessed Virgin Mary, 288 ff.
Charity, 30 ff., 151 f.
Chastity, 35 ff.
Christ, 32, 54, 66, 83 ff., 93 f., 109, 117, 135, 137 ff., 145, 152, 160 ff.
Church, 195 f.
Concupiscence, 10 f., 104
Creed, A Marian, After the manner of that of St. Athanasius, 298 f.

Daughter of the Lord, 90 ff.
Devils, 110, 143 f.
Diligence, 154 f.

Elizabeth, 33
Esther, 61, 116 f.

Fidelity, 86
Flower, Mary a, 114 ff., 118 ff.

Fruit of the womb of Mary, 160 ff.
Fullness of grace, 39 ff., 54 f., 63, 133 ff.

Generosity, 155 f.
Gentleness, 152 ff.
Gifts of the Holy Ghost, 48
Glory, 57, 74 f., 101 f., 128, 144 ff.
Grace, 37 ff.; Fourfold in Mary, 48 ff., 66 f., 101, 133 ff.

Handmaid of the Lord, 95 ff.
Hell, 11 ff., 191
Humility, 149 ff.

Illuminatrix, 21 ff., 111
Immortality, 122
Intercession, 56 f.

Jahel, 154
Jerusalem, 79, 147
Joy, 75 f.
Judith, 51, 78, 88, 143, 157 ff.
Justice, 85

Lady, 24 ff., 78
Liberality, 155 f.

Mary, Meanings of the name, 15 ff.
Mediatrix, 107 f.
Meekness, 152 ff.

Index

Mercy, 69, 84 f., 141
Merits, 130
Moon, 64 f., 156
Mother and virgin, 55 f., 92 ff.

Nabal, 141 f.
Name of Mary, 15 ff., 28 ff.

Odour, 73 f.
Original Sin, Mary's freedom from, 8 ff., 188

Peace-maker, 108 f.
Peace of mind, 105
Perfection, 71 f.
Perseverance, 32 f.
Piety, 69
Plenitudes, The nine, 63 ff.
Poverty, 33 f.
Psalter of the Blessed Virgin Mary, 199 ff.
Punishment, Eternal, Mary's freedom from, 11 ff.

Queen, Mary compared to a, 125 ff.
Queen of Heaven, 129 ff.

Rod, Mary a, 114 ff.
Ruth, 45, 87, 140

Salutation, The Angelical, 1 ff.
Sara, 57 f., 96, 151, 158
Seven virtues of Mary, against the seven capital vices, 149 ff.
Seven words of Mary, 51 ff.
Sin, Mary's freedom from, 5 ff.
Sisara, 154 f.
Sobriety, 35
Spouse of the Lord, 94 f.
Star of the Sea, 18 ff.
Susanna, 158 f.

Temperance, 156 f.

Virginity, 35 f., 43, 119, 126 f.

Printed in Great Britain
by Amazon.co.uk, Ltd.,
Marston Gate.